THEMATIC UNIT
Basketball

Written by Robert Smith

Teacher Created Materials, Inc.
6421 Industry Way
Westminster, CA 92683
www.teachercreated.com
©2002 Teacher Created Materials, Inc.
Made in U.S.A.
ISBN-0-7439-3103-3

Edited by
Karen Tam Froloff

Illustrated by
Bruce Hedges

Cover Art by
Brenda DiAntonis

The classroom teacher may reproduce copies of materials in this book for classroom use only. The reproduction of any part for an entire school or school system is strictly prohibited. No part of this publication may be transmitted, stored, or recorded in any form without written permission from the publisher.

Table of Contents

Introduction 3
   Center Court Sting by Matt Christopher (Little, Brown and Company, 1998) 5
     (Available in Canada, Little Brown; UK, Little Brown Ltd; AUS, Penguin)
     Summary—Sample Lesson Plan—Overview of Activities—Basketball Survey—The Rules of the Game—Basketball Equipment—Career Guidance—James Naismith: The Inventor of Basketball—Reading Comprehension Sheet—Nicknames—Dr. James Naismith's Original 13 Basketball Rules
   The Boxcar Children: The Basketball Mystery created by Gertrude Chandler Warner (Albert Whitman and Company, 1996) 21
     (Available in Canada, General Publishing; UK, Baker & Taylor International; AUS, Penguin)
     Summary—Sample Lesson Plan—Overview of Activities—It's a Girl's Game, Too—Wheelchair Basketball
   On the Court with . . . Michael Jordan by Matt Christopher (Little, Brown and Company, 1996) 28
     (Available in Canada, Little Brown; UK, Little Brown Ltd; AUS, Penguin)
     Summary—Sample Lesson Plan—Overview of Activities—Michael Jordan: The Greatest Player Ever—Reading Comprehension Sheet—Time Line: Michael Jordan and the United States
   Literature 36
     Matt Christopher: Sports Author—About the Author: Gertrude Chandler Warner—Meet the Boxcar Children
   Drama and Poetry 39
     Readers' Theater—The Poetry of Basketball—Write Your Own Poetry

Across the Curriculum
   Language Arts 47
     Basketball Terms—Basketball Lingo
   Math 49
     Computing Points per Game—Court Computations—Where the Money Is—Computing Shooting Percentages—Calculating Winning Percentages
   Social Studies/Geography 54
     Basketball Chronology—Where the Pros Play—U.S./Canada Map—What's In a Name?—The College Game—Olympic Basketball World Map—Research the NBA Greats
   Science 64
     For Every Action . . .—Dropping the Ball—Two Dropped Balls
   Health/P.E. 66
     Setting the Offense—Dribbling the Ball—Passing the Ball—Shooting the Ball—Shooting Games—Base Basketball—Basketball Etiquette
   Art 73
     Logos, Posters, and Uniforms

Culminating Activity 74
Unit Management 75
   Bulletin Board Ideas—Team Player Certificate
Bibliography 78
Answer Key 80

Introduction

Basketball is an exciting whole-language unit that delves into the history, rules, language, and science of basketball. These 80 pages are designed to immerse students in the multifaceted world of basketball through math, history, science, language, and especially literature. The literature choices for this unit are certain to excite the interest of your young readers and add to their store of knowledge as well. A wide variety of teaching strategies is employed throughout the text to motivate and maintain the high interest of students. These include hands-on activities, cooperative groups, team-building activities, and full-class instruction. In addition, there are attractive units introducing Readers' Theater, poetry writing, creative expression, science, and physical education. There is a strong unit on learning the skills of the game as well. At the core of this literature-based theme book are three excellent literature selections: *Center Court Sting* and *On the Court with . . . Michael Jordan* by Matt Christopher, and *The Boxcar Children: The Basketball Mystery* created by Gertrude Chandler Warner.

This thematic unit includes the following:

- ❑ **literature selections**—summaries of three books related to the topic of basketball

- ❑ **fine arts**—suggestions for activities in the visual arts

- ❑ **planning guidance**—sequenced lessons and activities to provide a natural flow of study, which increases understanding of the various concepts of basketball

- ❑ **bulletin boards**—suggestions and instructions for content-related bulletin boards

- ❑ **curriculum connections**—activities that interweave language arts, math, social studies, science, health/P.E., and art with basketball

- ❑ **culminating activities**—experiences that allow students to apply their learning

- ❑ **resources**—bibliography and lists of books and sources of materials, specifically related to basketball

- ❑ **answer key**—answers for activities in this unit

> **To keep this valuable resource intact so that it can be used year after year, you may wish to punch holes in the pages and store them in a three-ring binder.**

© Teacher Created Materials, Inc.

Introduction (cont.)

Why a Balanced Approach?

The strength of a whole-language approach is that it involves children in using all modes of communication—reading, writing, listening, observing, illustrating, and doing. Communication skills are interconnected and integrated into lessons that emphasize the whole of language. Balancing this approach is our knowledge that every whole—including individual words—is composed of parts, and directed study of those parts can help a student to master the whole. Experience and research tell us that regular attention to phonics, other word-attack skills, and spelling develops reading mastery, thereby fulfilling the unity of the whole-language experience. The child is thus led to read, write, spell, speak, and listen confidently in response to a literature experience introduced by the teacher. In these ways, language skills grow rapidly, stimulated by direct practice, involvement, and interest in the topic at hand.

Why Thematic Planning?

One very useful tool for implementing a balanced language program is thematic planning. By choosing a theme with correlating literature selections for a unit of study, a teacher can plan activities throughout the day that lead to a cohesive, in-depth study of the topic. Students will be practicing and applying their skills in meaningful contexts. Consequently, they will tend to learn and retain more. Both teachers and students will be freed from a day that is broken into unrelated segments of isolated drill and practice.

Why Cooperative Learning?

Besides academic skills and content, students need to learn social skills. This area of development cannot be taken for granted. Students must learn to work cooperatively in groups in order to function well in modern society. Group activities should be a regular part of school life, and teachers should consciously include social objectives as well as academic objectives in their planning. For example, a group working together to solve a problem may need to select a leader. Teachers should make clear to the students the qualities of good leader-follower group interaction just as they would state and monitor the academic goals of the project.

Four Basic Components of Cooperative Learning

1. *In cooperative learning, all group members need to work together to accomplish the task.*

2. *Cooperative learning groups should be heterogeneous.*

3. *Cooperative learning activities need to be designed so that each student contributes to the group, and individual group members can be assessed on their performance.*

4. *Cooperative learning teams need to know the social as well as the academic objectives of a lesson.*

Center Court Sting

by Matt Christopher

Summary

Center Court Sting is a fast-paced basketball story centered around a junior high team, the Rangers. The main character is Daren McCall, a good basketball player with a fierce temper and a poor attitude. He insults other members of the team if they don't perform well. He gets on the team center, Lou Bettman, when he has several bad games. He argues a call with the referees and gets a technical foul, which contributes to the Rangers losing a game. He treats the team manager, Andy Higgins, like a servant. He even blows up at his best friend, Lynn Mayes, when Lynn doesn't agree with him. A locker room prank exacerbates the conflict between Daren and Lou and the entire team is in turmoil.

Daren's friend and neighbor, Judy, asks him to teach her little brother, Gary, how to play basketball. Daren criticizes the boy's efforts and makes fun of him, causing the younger boy to quit in frustration.

Daren's attitude begins to change when he realizes that he has angered all of his teammates, including his best friend. His coach tells Daren that he may either bench him or drop him from the team if he doesn't become a team player. Daren then finds out that Lou's mother is very sick and has been in the hospital for several weeks, which accounts for Lou's distractions on the court. Judy chews him out for the way he treated Gary and his father gives him some tough advice about being understanding with Gary and his teammates. Daren begins to make a conscious effort to become a team player as the team practices for the big game coming up against the Rebels. He works hard to do the drills the coach teaches them and to find ways on the court to help out on defense, to look for ways to help his teammates score, and to become a more selfless player, in general.

Daren finds out that the team manager was responsible for the pranks that nearly brought Lou and Daren to blows. Daren realizes that his attitude had been partly responsible and he doesn't get angry with Andy and even accepts his apology. Daren gets another chance to help Gary and both Gary and Judy come to the big game against the Rebels.

As the game draws to an end, the team learns to play with a newfound cohesiveness and Daren finds pride and success by becoming a team leader on and off the court.

Center Court Sting (cont.)

The outline below is a suggested plan for using the various activities and ideas that are presented in this unit. You should adapt these ideas to fit your own classroom situation.

Sample Lesson Plan

Day 1
- Read Chapters 1 and 2.
- Conduct SSR (Sustained Silent Reading).
- Discuss Daren's attitude toward his teammates. How does he get along with the coach and other players? What kind of an attitude does he have on the court? How do his teammates respond to Daren?
- Conduct a Basketball Survey (Setting the Stage, #4).
- Begin a reading journal (Enjoying the Book, #4).
- Review the Rules of the Game (Setting the Stage, #6).

Day 2
- Read Chapters 3 and 4.
- Conduct SSR.
- Discuss friendship. Is Lynn a good friend, even if he doesn't agree with Daren? How do Shawn and Lynn demonstrate their loyalty in the cafeteria?
- Continue the reading journal.
- Teach the game, Base Basketball (Enjoying the Book, #3).
- Do For Every Action . . . activity (Enjoying the Book, #5).
- Do the Basketball Lingo activity (Enjoying the Book, #8, #9).

Day 3
- Read Chapters 5 and 6.
- Conduct SSR.
- Discuss what Daren did wrong in teaching Gary. How should he have helped the younger boy?
- Continue the reading journal.
- Do the Dropping the Ball activity (Enjoying the Book, #6).
- Introduce writing topic (Enjoying the Book, #10).

Day 4
- Read Chapters 7 and 8.
- Conduct SSR.
- Discuss why the Rangers lose the game. Were the Blazers just a better team or were the Rangers not playing together? What should the coach have done to make this team better? Should the coach bench Daren or drop him from the team?
- Continue the reading journal.
- Do the Two Dropped Balls activity (Enjoying the Book, #7).
- Read James Naismith: The Inventor of Basketball (Extending the Book, #3).
- Continue writing topic.

Day 5
- Read Chapters 9 through 11.
- Conduct SSR.
- Discuss Daren's change of attitude. What changed the way he thought about Lou? Who had the most influence on Daren's attitude—Judy, his dad, the coach, Lynn, Lou, or the team? Is winning important? Why?
- Conclude the reading journal.
- Do Elements of a Story (Enjoying the Book, #11).
- Learn more about the author (Extending the Book, #8).
- Read Basketball Chronology (Extending the Book, #6).
- Discuss Basketball Etiquette (Extending the Book, #9).
- Write Point of View diary entry (Extending the Book, #10).

Center Court Sting

Overview of Activities

Setting the Stage

1. Set the mood by asking students to describe the best basketball game they ever saw or ever played in.

2. Read the first chapter from *Center Court Sting* aloud to the class to excite their interest in the book.

3. Ask each student who plays on an organized basketball team to make a list of pertinent facts about his or her team and his or her league. You can choose the local NBA team to discuss, too. These facts should include:

   - uniforms and sponsors
   - number of teams
   - names of the best teams
   - names of the best players
   - specific rules each team must follow
   - the number of players on each team
   - who coaches the teams
   - who can join the team
   - whether every player gets into every game
   - other important information

4. Conduct a survey of students in your class about the game of basketball. Use the **Basketball Survey** form (page 11). Help students compile the results of the survey on a class chart. Ask students to create a bar graph to visually express the survey results.

5. Conduct a general discussion with students about the basic rules of the game of basketball. Discuss favorite players and teams. Ask students to describe their feelings about the game and the aspects of the game that they like or dislike.

6. Review the **Rules of the Game** (pages 12 and 13) and **Basketball Equipment** (page 14) with your students. Students should then divide into pairs. One student tries to explain how the game of basketball is played to the other student as if that student had no prior knowledge of the game. Students should then switch roles and repeat the process.

Enjoying the Book

1. Read the book *Center Court Sting* over a period of about five days. Your students should read about two chapters a day during SSR.

2. Read **Setting the Offense** (page 66) so those less-knowledgeable students have a sense of the players' positions on the court. Ask various students playing on teams to define their own roles as guards, forwards, or centers.

Center Court Sting

Overview of Activities (cont.)

Enjoying the Book (cont.)

3. Introduce the game **Base Basketball** (page 71) to the students. Have the students read the game rules and then set up one or two P.E. periods devoted to the game. An advantage of this game is that dribbling is not a required skill and the shooter is not guarded.

4. Have students keep a reading journal while they read this book.

   Each entry should record:

   —the number of pages read

   —new vocabulary words

   —impressions and reactions to each chapter section

   —responses to Daren's behaviors and attitudes

   —whether they empathized with Daren or disapproved of his attitude

5. Do the science activity **For Every Action . . .** (page 64). This activity helps students recognize how the ball responds when it is bounced off a floor or wall. This can be done as a combined science/P.E. activity.

6. Help students do the **Dropping the Ball** activity (page 65). You may need to borrow several balls from other classrooms or ask students to bring a variety of balls from home. You will also need several measuring sticks or tapes. Students should notice that one way to get a high bounce is to have a ball filled with air.

7. Do the follow-up science activity **Two Dropped Balls** (page 65) with the entire class if you can borrow enough basketballs and tennis balls or other small balls. This activity demonstrates the transfer of energy.

8. Review **Basketball Terms** (page 47) and **Basketball Lingo** (page 48). Ask students to use some of these expressions in their own play-by-play account of one period of a basketball game. They may create an imaginary game or describe a game they played in or watched. Students should feel free to add terms or to make up their own lingo.

9. Ask students to illustrate several expressions from **Basketball Lingo** (page 48). For example, a "brick" could be illustrated as a rectangular basketball that looked like a brick. A "skywalk" might show a player walking on the sky. Have students do several illustrated expressions. A cartoon style of illustration is often effective. These make a great bulletin board display.

10. Tell students to write an essay as a personal response to literature on the following prompt:

    If you were playing on a basketball team with a player as critical of other people as Daren was, how would you handle the situation? Would you try to ignore him? Would you quit the team? Would you try to change the player? Explain your position. Provide reasons and examples from *Center Court Sting* and your own experiences.

#3103 Thematic Unit—Basketball © Teacher Created Materials, Inc.

Center Court Sting

Overview of Activities *(cont.)*

Enjoying the Book *(cont.)*

11. Create a chart with your students indicating the elements of a story similar to the one below.

Elements of a Story

Setting of the story
- Where (country/city/rural/school)
- When (time period)

Major characters
- One or two descriptive facts about each one

Lesser characters
- One or two descriptive facts about each one

Plot
- Story line of the book in about seven to ten brief sentences

Problem
- What is the basic problem in the book for the main character? Express this problem in one sentence.

Climax
- What one event in the story does everything lead up to and then lead to a resolution?

Ending
- What is the denouement? How does the story end—for the main character, especially?

Feeling
- Is the general tone of the book depressing, uplifting, happy, sad, grim, joyful, funny, light, or serious? Choose the appropriate descriptive words.

Extending the Book

1. Divide your class into teams of three to five students each. Discuss the **Readers' Theater** (pages 39 through 41) and use the instructions on converting text into a script. Have each team choose a chapter or a scene from *Center Court Sting* to convert to dramatic format. Then have each drama team presents their Readers' Theater to the class audience.

2. Read *The Great Brain at the Academy* (see Bibliography, page 78) chapter 10, entitled: "Basketball and the Bishop." This chapter gives an interesting description of basketball as it was played in the formative years before 1900. The story is set in Utah in 1897. Create a script for Readers Theater based on the game played in this chapter. Practice and perform the script for the class.

3. Ask students to read **James Naismith: The Inventor of Basketball** (page 16). Have students do the **Reading Comprehension Sheet** (page 17). Remind them to find and underline the answers in the text. This procedure attunes them to the processes of reading for meaning and information.

Overview of Activities (cont.)

Extending the Book (cont.)

4. Read **Dr. James Naismith's Original 13 Basketball Rules** (pages 19 and 20) with the class. Ask students to do the activity telling which rules have changed and which have remained the same.

5. Ask students to write a compare-and-contrast essay describing the differences between early basketball and the way the game is played today. Students should be able to write two very detailed paragraphs.

6. Read **Basketball Chronology** (pages 54 and 55) with your class. This is a basketball time line of changes and events in the game. Discuss how the United States and the world have changed over the last century in terms of transportation and lifestyle. Have students mark on the chronology or on a separate paper some of the important events in United States and world history since 1891.

7. Ms. Cass, the English teacher, gives Daren a hard time when he isn't paying attention in English class. Have students describe an experience they had in class when a teacher got upset with their behavior or work. Have them describe their feelings and explain why they were in trouble. Remind them to be completely honest with themselves.

8. Use the **Matt Christopher: Sports Author** biography (page 36) and the Matt Christopher books listed in the **Bibliography** (page 79) to encourage students to read other books by the author. Most public libraries have many copies of Mr. Christopher's work because of its popularity. Encourage students to read one or more of his books, either with a basketball theme or some other sport that appeals to individual tastes.

9. Read about **Basketball Etiquette** (page 72). Ask students to do the creative writing activity on losing your temper. Encourage teams of students to do the role playing activity about controlling temper and providing leadership.

10. Ask students to keep or create a diary of a basketball game— using point of view. A student could write the diary entry from the point of view of a specific player on the team. The student would then give the same information from the point of view of a teammate, a player from the opposing team, a referee, a coach, a parent, a sibling, or a friend. If students have trouble creating a situation, allow them to use the incidents between Daren and Carl in the first chapter when Daren gets the technical foul.

Center Court Sting

Basketball Survey

Directions: Fill out the survey and compare it with those of your classmates. Then record the results in the table below.

What is your favorite sport? _____

Do you like to play basketball? _____

Do you like to watch basketball? _____

What is your favorite NBA team? _____

Who is your favorite NBA player? _____

Who is your basketball hero? _____

Have you ever been to an NBA game? _____

Do you play organized basketball in any league? _____

Would you want to play basketball when you grow up? _____

Who is the greatest player of all time? _____

Directions: Record the results of your survey on the table below.

Table of Preferences

Favorite sport
- Basketball _____
- Baseball _____
- Football _____
- Soccer _____
- Other _____

Like to play basketball
- ❏ Yes   ❏ No

Like to watch basketball
- ❏ Yes   ❏ No

Favorite NBA team _____

Favorite NBA player _____

Basketball hero _____

Attend NBA games
- ❏ Yes   ❏ No

Play organized basketball in any league
- ❏ Yes   ❏ No

Greatest player of all time _____

Center Court Sting

The Rules of the Game

Basketball is a very complex sport with a large number of rules. Listed here are the basic rules that apply to all or most levels of the sport from youth leagues through the pros.

- There are five players on a team. A coach may substitute one player for another. The substitute reports to the scorer and waits until the clock stops and an official waves in the new player.

- A player cannot carry the ball or walk with the ball. The player must dribble the ball if he or she moves or lose possession of the ball to the other team.

- A player cannot dribble the ball, stop dribbling, and then dribble again. This is called "double dribble" and the ball goes to the other team.

- The ball must be dribbled with the fingertips. It may not be slapped by the palm. The ball may not be held by the hand under the ball, dribbled, and held under the ball again. This is called "palming the ball."

- A defensive player may not reach in between the arms to try to steal the ball. "Reaching in" is a foul.

- A player may not deliberately trip, shove, push, hit, or injure another player. These are all personal fouls.

- A player may not pin a ball which has been shot against the backboard. He may not intercept a ball on the way down toward the basket or in the basket. This is called "goaltending" and it is a foul.

- A player dribbling the ball may not charge into another player who is not moving. This foul is called "charging." (If both players are moving, the referee will decide who deserves the foul.)

- A player may not reach in and try to grab a ball from a rebounder who has possession of the ball. If a ball goes out of bounds, it goes to the team that did not have possession of the ball. The team that last touched the ball loses possession.

- If a ball is mistakenly shot into the opposition's basket, that team gets the goal.

- A free throw for a foul shot is worth one point.

- A field goal is worth two points.

- A goal made beyond the three-point line is worth three points.

The Rules of the Game (cont.)

- A shot clock is used in most leagues. The 24-second clock in the NBA requires that a shot be attempted within 24 seconds or the ball goes to the other team. (Some leagues use 30-second or 35-second clocks.)

- A jump ball is used to begin a game and sometimes in cases of disputed possession. In a jump ball, two players face each other in the circle at center court and jump when the referee throws the ball into the air. Each of the two jumpers tries to tip the ball to a player on his team. A jumper may not grab the ball himself. An alternate possession pointer is used in many leagues for cases of disputed possession.

- A whistle blown by an official stops the play and the clock.

- An offensive player is not permitted to stay in the painted area called the key for more than three seconds. If he does, his team loses possession of the ball. (The player may move in and out of the area but may not stay longer than three seconds at any one time.)

- A team has only 10 seconds to move the ball over the division line at center court into the opponent's half of the court. If the offensive team fails to get the ball over the line, it loses possession of the ball.

- A team may not move the ball back over the center court division line into its half of the court once any team has crossed the line. That team loses possession of the ball unless the other team last touched the ball (in an attempted steal, for example).

- A team may attempt to steal the ball from the offensive team, but it may not make bodily contact.

- A player must make a throw-in from the sidelines or endlines within five seconds. If the player fails to throw it in within five seconds, then the team loses possession of the ball.

- A player or coach who argues a call with a referee, who demonstrates bad sportsmanship, or who uses excessive force will receive a technical foul. The other team will shoot a foul shot alone on the court and get possession of the ball. Two technical fouls or extreme violence requires ejection from the game.

- A player with five fouls, personal or technical, must be removed from the game. (The NBA allows six fouls.)

- An offensive player with the ball, who steps out of bounds or on the line or who allows the ball to touch the line or go out of bounds, loses possession of the ball to the other team.

- A ball is not out of bounds if it is still in the air and has not touched the line or floor out of bounds.

Center Court Sting

Basketball Equipment

Basketball does not require a lot of equipment. All you need is a backboard, a hoop, a net, a basketball, and a hard, flat surface. Many parks have basketball courts for you to play on. Then all you need is the basketball.

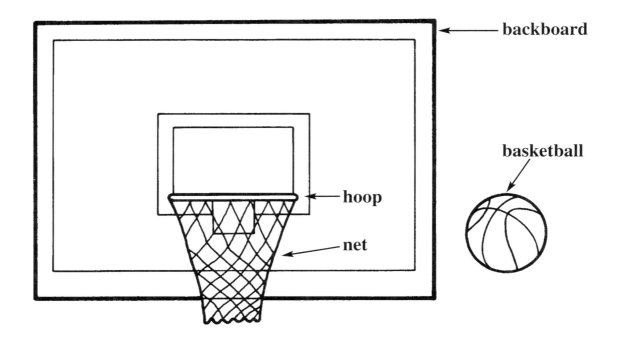

Basketball Court

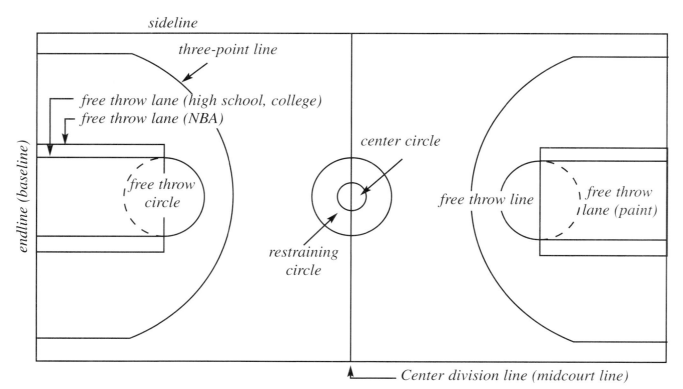

Center Court Sting

Career Guidance

Matt Christopher knew he wanted to be a writer by the time he was 14 years old. Sports careers seem attractive and millions of children play basketball but only a few hundred actually make it to the NBA and only a handful of them will become superstars. Use this page to help you determine some serious and reasonable career choices.

Career Choices

List three school subjects you like:

_____ _____ _____

List four interests or hobbies that you do outside of school (stamp collecting, video games, computer use, playing an instrument, etc.):

_____ _____
_____ _____

List four activities that you would like to learn (speak Italian, cook, play an instrument, etc.):

_____ _____
_____ _____

List some sports you play alone or on teams:
_____

List some subjects you like to read about:

_____ _____ _____

Do you like to build with your hands? _____
Do you like to learn about new things? _____
Do you like surprises? _____
Do you like to work alone or with a group? _____
Who is your hero in life and why? _____
_____

What is your proudest accomplishment? _____
_____

Do you like physical activity? _____
Do you like to draw or paint? _____
Do you like to do academic work (schoolwork)? _____

Career Goals

List four careers you think you would like and be good at and describe why.

Career	Reason
1. _____	_____
2. _____	_____
3. _____	_____
4. _____	_____

Center Court Sting

James Naismith: The Inventor of Basketball

James Naismith was in a quandary. It was winter and he needed to keep the young men in his physical education class active.

He was an instructor at the School for Christian Workers, which trained leaders for the Young Men's Christian Association. His boss, Luther Gulick, had suggested that James create a game that would keep the young athletes at the school energized and exercised throughout the winter. Baseball, soccer, football, and rugby were all summer games but winter was cold, snowy, and long in Springfield, Massachusetts. The school gym had a hardwood indoor floor and Naismith didn't want the rough and tumble play of soccer, lacrosse, or football, all of which he tried to modify to meet his needs but without success.

James remembered a contest he and his fellow rugby players used to have when he attended McGill College in his native country, Canada. As they ran around the gym floor, players had tried to toss a ball into a box in the center of the gym. Naismith combined this idea with a child's game called "Duck on a Rock" which involved throwing objects at a small rock sitting on a fence or a large boulder.

Finally, Naismith decided on a soccer ball and an elevated goal that could be attached to the two balcony railings at each end of the indoor gym. With the help of the janitor who found two peach baskets to use as goals, he attached these wooden crates to the balcony railings. Four days before Christmas in 1891, James pinned the 13 rules of "Basket Ball" to the school bulletin board and invited the students to try out his game.

Naismith divided his class of 18 men into two nine-man teams and explained that the object of the game was to throw the ball into the peach crate, which the opposing team was defending. The ball could only be advanced by passing. A player could not run with the ball. Players were not allowed to hit other players or to hit the ball with their fists. The janitor kept a ladder nearby to retrieve the ball after a goal was made.

The game was an instant success. The young men loved the game and its popularity spread fast. Almost immediately, the game was adopted by a group of neighborhood teachers. Soon, other schools and colleges throughout the nation were playing the game.

Eventually, open-ended nets, rims, and backboards replaced the peach baskets. Dribbling the ball was required and teams were gradually reduced to five players. Games with scores like 2 to 2, 5 to 1, and 15 to 13 were common in the early years, but the game was sped up and higher scores became the norm. James Naismith died in 1939. The Basketball Hall of Fame in Springfield, Massachusetts, is named in his honor.

Center Court Sting

Reading Comprehension Sheet

Directions: Circle the best answer for the following questions, based on the information you read about James Naismith on page 16.

1. Which country was James Naismith's native home?
   A. Brazil
   B. Canada
   C. United States
   D. Mexico

2. How many players were on a team in Naismith's original game?
   A. 6
   B. 9
   C. 5
   D. 12

3. What did James use for goals in his new game?
   A. boxes
   B. nets
   C. a balcony
   D. peach baskets

4. In whose honor is the Basketball Hall of Fame named?
   A. Wilt Chamberlain
   B. James Naismith
   C. Luther Gulick
   D. Michael Jordan

5. What does it mean to be "in a quandary"?
   A. stuck in the snow
   B. to have a problem to solve
   C. caught in the mud
   D. hurt by a fall

6. Who suggested that James Naismith create a game?
   A. his students
   B. Luther Gulick
   C. the janitor
   D. rugby players

7. What kind of ball did Naismith use for his new game?
   A. soccer ball
   B. rugby ball
   C. football
   D. baseball

8. What year was basketball invented?
   A. 1891
   B. 1939
   C. 1981
   D. 1892

9. What did the janitor have to do after each goal?
   A. referee the game
   B. clean the ball
   C. sweep the gym
   D. get the ball out of the basket

10. In what month was basketball invented?
    A. January
    B. September
    C. March
    D. December

Center Court Sting

Nicknames

Basketball players have some of the most unusual and descriptive nicknames in sports. Many times they are given because of the person's playing style or personality.

Directions: Read the names of the players on this list and their monikers. Then, on another sheet of paper, choose 10 nicknames and tell why that player might have been given that nickname. Illustrate several of the nicknames such as a "Magic" ballplayer or an "Iceman" shooting.

Player	Nickname
Bob Cousy	"The Houdini of the Hardwood"
Julius Erving	"Dr. J"
Clyde Drexler	"The Glide"
Nate Archibald	"Tiny"
Walt Frazier	"Clyde"
George Gervin	"The Iceman"
John Havlicek	"Hondo"
Elvin Hayes	"The Big E"
Pete Maravich	"Pistol Pete"
Earl Monroe	"The Pearl"
Hakeem Olajuwon	"The Dream"
Karl Malone	"The Mailman"
Robert Parrish	"The Chief"
Cedric Maxwell	"Cornbread"
Shaquille O'Neal	"Shaq"
David Robinson	"The Admiral"
Isiah Thomas	"Zeke"
Jerry West	"Mr. Clutch"
Wilt Chamberlain	"The Stilt"
Oscar Robertson	"The Big O"
Vinnie Johnson	"The Microwave"
Freddy Brown	"Downtown"
Bill Bradley	"Dollar Bill"
Dennis Rodman	"Worm"
Eric Floyd	"Sleepy"
Anfernee Hardaway	"Penny"
Kenny Anderson	"The Kid"
Tyrone Bogues	"Muggsy"
Earvin Johnson	"Magic"
Michael Jordan	"Air Jordan"
Xavier McDaniel	"The X-Man"
Rik Smits	"Dunking Dutchman"

Dr. James Naismith's Original 13 Basketball Rules

Dr. James Naismith published his original 13 rules for "Basket Ball" in the *Triangle*, a newspaper for YMCA School of Christian Workers on January 15, 1892, about a month after the first game was played.

Directions: Read the object of the game and Dr. Naismith's 13 rules. Then, on the following page, note changes to the rules as the game is generally played today. Try to find the three rules that have stayed about the same.

Basket Ball Rules

The object of the game is to put the ball into your opponent's goal. This may be done by throwing the ball from any part of the grounds, with one or two hands, under the following conditions and rules.

1. The ball may be thrown in any direction with one or both hands.
2. The ball may be batted in any direction with one or both hands but never with the fist.
3. A player cannot run with the ball. The player must throw it from the spot on which he catches it, allowances to be made for a man who catches the ball when running if he tries to stop.
4. The ball must be held by the hands. The arms or body must not be used for holding it.
5. No shouldering, holding, pushing, tripping, or striking, in any way, the person of an opponent shall be allowed. The first infringement of this rule by any player shall count as a foul. The second infringement shall disqualify him until the next goal is made. If there was evident intent to injure the person, it shall disqualify him for the whole of the game, no substitute allowed.
6. A foul is striking the ball with the fist, violation of Rules Three, Four, and such as described in Rule Five.
7. If either side makes three consecutive fouls, it shall count as a goal for the opponents. (Consecutive means without the opponents in the meantime making a foul.)
8. A goal shall be made when the ball is thrown or batted from the grounds into the basket and stays there, providing those defending the goal do not touch or disturb the goal. If the ball rests on the edge and the opponent moves the basket, it shall count as a goal.
9. When the ball goes out of bounds, it shall be thrown into the field of play by the person who last touched it.
   He has a right to hold it unmolested for five seconds.
   In case of a dispute, the umpire shall throw it straight into the field.
   The thrower-in is allowed five seconds. If he holds it longer, it shall go to the opponent.
   If any side persists in delaying the game, the umpire shall call a foul on that side.
10. The umpire shall be the judge of the men and shall note the fouls and notify the referee when three consecutive fouls have been made. He shall have power to disqualify men according to Rule Five.
11. The referee shall be judge of the ball and shall decide when the ball is in play, in bounds, to which side it belongs, and shall keep the time. He shall decide when a goal has been made and keep account of the goals, with any other duties that are usually performed by a referee.
12. The time shall be two fifteen-minute halves, with five minutes rest in between.
13. The side making the most goals in that time shall be declared the winner. In the case of a draw, the game may, by agreement of the captains, be continued until another goal is made.

Center Court Sting

Dr. James Naismith's Original 13 Basketball Rules (cont.)

Changes to the Rules

Rule 1 _____
_____

Rule 2 _____
_____

Rule 3 _____
_____

Rule 4 _____
_____

Rule 5 _____
_____

Rule 6 _____
_____

Rule 7 _____
_____

Rule 8 _____
_____

Rule 9 _____
_____

Rule 10 _____
_____

Rule 11 _____
_____

Rule 12 _____
_____

Rule 13 _____
_____

The Boxcar Children: The Basketball Mystery

Created by Gertrude Chandler Warner

Summary

The Boxcar Children: The Basketball Mystery begins with the four Alden children playing basketball on their driveway. We quickly meet Henry, the oldest, who is in high school. Jessie, at 12, is the second oldest. Violet is a little younger and Benny is six years old. Their Korean cousin, Soo Lee, is five.

The kids just finished a two-on-two game when two college-age youths show up. The Nettleton twins, Buzz and Tipper, have become locally famous for their high school basketball careers and their basketball success in college where Tipper won a "Most Valuable Player" trophy, a sore point with her twin brother. The twins who are relatives of the family and are staying with the Aldens while making some community service appearances, helping to dedicate a new sports arena for children, and coaching some younger players.

The twins get so involved with their appearances at various functions that they seem disorganized and miss some crucial practices with the teams they are going to coach. The situation is compounded by the obvious jealousy of Frank Fowler and Courtney Post, two local coaches, who are upset at all of the attention the twins are getting and at the fact the twins had eclipsed their high school records when they played in Greenfield.

Despite several setbacks and disappointments for the twins, they put on a very successful basketball clinic at the Aldens and try to give credit to Frank and Courtney for their help. In the course of the clinic, Tipper finds that her trophy is missing. She knows that both Buzz and Courtney have been envious since she won the trophy.

In the final chapters, Buzz finds the team he's coaching, the Blazers, being penalized by Frank's unfair refereeing but teaches his players how to handle adversity and still win. Tipper coaches the Fast Breakers to victory over Courtney's team by using all of her players effectively while Courtney relies only on a few top players.

The mystery of Tipper's missing trophy is solved when one of Tipper's players, Patsy, admits that she took it. Frank and Courtney also admit to their discomfort over the attention given to the twins by the local media.

Two themes are central to the book. The jealousy of Frank, Courtney, Patsy, and Buzz leads to spiteful words, distrust, and improper behavior. A model of good sportsmanship is also fostered. Helping every child be a better ballplayer, treating players individually but fairly, and responding to bad luck with responsible behavior are highlighted in this story.

The Boxcar Children: The Basketball Mystery (cont.)

The outline below is a suggested plan for using the various activities and ideas that are presented in this unit. You should adapt these ideas to fit your own classroom situation.

Sample Lesson Plan

Day 1
- Read Chapter 1 aloud to class (Setting the Stage, #2).
- Read Chapters 1 and 2.
- Conduct SSR (Sustained Silent Reading).
- Discuss why Frank Fowler and Courtney Post don't seem very friendly with the twins. What do you think Patsy was doing next to Tipper's bed? Why are the Nettleton twins famous? What trophy did Tipper win? How does Buzz feel about the trophy?
- Discuss visits from relatives (Setting the Stage, #3).
- Begin a reading journal (Enjoying the Book, #9).
- Write about twin experiences (Setting the Stage, #4).
- Begin basketball skills (Enjoying the Book, #5).

Day 2
- Read Chapters 3 and 4.
- Conduct SSR.
- Discuss Courtney's attitude toward Tipper. Why are Tipper and Courtney arguing? What do you think happened to the storage room key? Why were the Blazers upset at Buzz? What does Tom do at the new sports center? How would you feel if you were Tipper and Buzz?
- Continue the reading journal.
- Introduce Poetry (Enjoying the Book, #2).
- Continue writing about twin experiences.
- Continue basketball skills.

Day 3
- Read Chapters 5 and 6.
- Conduct SSR.
- Discuss what happened to Tipper's trophy. How did Jessie and Tipper know it was missing? How do the twins try to reduce the ill feeling Frank and Courtney have toward them? Who do you think took the trophy?
- Continue the reading journal.
- Write Poetry (Enjoying the Book, #4).
- Continue basketball skills.
- Introduce passing practice (Enjoying the Book, #5, #7).

Day 4
- Read Chapters 7 and 8.
- Conduct SSR.
- Discuss the Blazer game against the Hot Shots. Describe what happened during the game.
  How did Buzz handle the referee's poor calls? How did Buzz teach his players to handle the bad calls? Why is Tipper going to coach the Fast Breakers alone? Who is Courtney coaching?
- Continue the reading journal.
- Introduce Shooting the Ball (Enjoying the Book, #5, #6).
- Continue poetry writing.
- Introduce Poetry in Two Voices (Enjoying the Book, #3).
- Read about the author (Extending the Book, #1).
- Continue dribbling, passing, and shooting practice.

Day 5
- Read Chapters 9 and 10.
- Conduct SSR.
- Discuss the game between the Fast Breakers and the Blue Stars. Describe the action of the game. Explain the difference between Tipper's style of coaching and Courtney's. What did you think of the story? Would you like to read other books in the series?
- Conclude the reading journal.
- Do Elements of a Story (Enjoying the Book, #10).
- Read the introduction to the Boxcar Children (Extending the Book, #2).
- Encourage students to read other Boxcar books (Extending the Book, #3).
- Read Wheelchair Basketball (Extending the Book, #7).
- Do Chair Shooting (Extending the Book, #8).
- Write Response to Literature (Extending the Book, #9).

The Boxcar Children: The Basketball Mystery

Overview of Activities

Setting the Stage

1. Before reading the book, ask students to anticipate what the book may be about judging by the title and the cover.

2. Read the first chapter from *The Boxcar Children: The Basketball Mystery* aloud to the class to spark their interest in the book.

3. Lead a discussion about going to visit friends or having friends or relatives come to stay for a short time. Have students list the positive and negative aspects of having other people stay at their homes.

4. Tipper and Buzz are twins. Encourage each student to imagine that he or she is a twin to another person. Have students write a narrative in which they describe the experiences of being a twin. Real twins can describe their experiences and give some of the good and bad points of being a twin.

5. Remind students that Daren helped Gary learn how to play basketball. Ask students who helped them with the game and why it feels good to learn from someone older and more skilled.

Enjoying the Book

1. Have students read *The Boxcar Children: The Basketball Mystery* during SSR over a period of five days at a rate of about two chapters per day.

2. Read **The Poetry of Basketball** (page 42) and some sports poems to the class from *Opening Days/Sports Poems* or any of the poetry selections listed in the bibliography (page 78).

3. Encourage students to respond to the feelings and the language flow of the poems. Do the **Poetry in Two Voices** section (page 42).

4. Write poetry. Use the **Write Your Own Poetry** section (pages 43 through 46) in this book to guide students in writing cinquains, diamantes, I like…, and I wish... poems.

5. Read about **Dribbling the Ball, Passing the Ball**, and **Shooting the Ball** (pages 67 through 69) with students. Conduct a week or two of basketball drills based on the skills of dribbling, passing, and shooting.

6. As students become more proficient in basketball, introduce the **Shooting Games** (page 70). Most of these activities can be done in small groups. Borrow enough basketballs from other classes and ask students to bring in basketballs they have at home.

7. Encourage students to do the passing practice activities detailed on page 68. These could be done at recess, during free play, or during structured P.E. time. Students can practice these drills on their own time, as well.

8. Read about lay-ups (page 69) with your students. Do each activity for two days. Students will practice basic lay-ups for two days and then play games of one-on-one for two days. The last two days will be spent on fast breaks and practicing the earlier skills. These were some of the activities Tipper and Buzz did with the Fast Breakers and the Blazers.

© Teacher Created Materials, Inc.

The Boxcar Children: The Basketball Mystery

Overview of Activities *(cont.)*

Enjoying the Book *(cont.)*

9. Expect students to keep a reading journal, as they did with *Center Court Sting*, while they read this book.

   Each entry should record the following:

   - the number of pages read
   - new vocabulary words
   - impressions and reactions to each chapter section
   - responses to Frank and Courtney's behaviors and attitudes
   - every action or event that seemed unusual or mysterious
   - every instance of jealousy
   - favorite characters in the book

10. Create a chart with students indicating the **Elements of a Story** similar to the one they did with *Center Court Sting*. Use the outline on page 9.

Extending the Book

1. Read the biography of Gertrude Chandler Warner (page 37) with your students. Use this piece as an introduction to the original book and to other books in the series. **Meet the Boxcar Children** (page 38) could be used for the same purpose.

2. *The Boxcar Children*, which introduced the series, is a book that appeals strongly to most readers of both genders. Use the book as a read-aloud for your class. Find as many copies of the book as you can so that some of your students can track with you as you read. Reading aloud to students is a very effective way of encouraging reading and arousing interest in books.

3. Public libraries usually have many copies of *The Boxcar Children* series. Encourage each child in your class to choose one of the books listed in the bibliography (page 79) to read in their SSR and homework time. Award a certificate to each student who reads and reports on several of these books.

4. Tipper and Buzz were college students. Have students do **The College Game** (page 59).

5. Tipper and Buzz were proud to come home and coach younger players. Write a Response-to-Literature Essay entitled "Coaching Younger Players." Explain why having older students act as coaches for younger players could be a great experience for both the coaches and the players. Use examples from *The Basketball Mystery* and your personal experiences.

The Boxcar Children: The Basketball Mystery

Overview of Activities *(cont.)*

Extending the Book *(cont.)*

6. Read **It's a Girl's Game, Too** (page 26) about women's basketball with your students. Compare how girls play the game now and how it used to be played. Encourage several students of both genders to research other aspects of women's basketball and to share their findings with the class.

7. Read **Wheelchair Basketball** (page 27) with your class. Ask students to share any experiences they had have had in playing with children who were physically challenged.

8. Tipper Nettleton used chair shooting as a technique to help her players learn to follow through on their shots. Organize teams of about six students each to try the **Chair Shooting** activity on page 27. Students will acquire some empathy for wheelchair-bound schoolmates and also develop some basketball skills.

9. In the leagues that the Boxcar Children are playing in, every child is supposed to play in every game. The Fast Breakers actually win their game against Courtney's team because everyone has a chance to play. Write a Response-to-Literature Essay entitled "Who Gets to Play." Explain why you think only the best players should play or why every player should play even if it means the team loses the game.

10. Buzz and Tipper are winning basketball players, but they aren't willing to win at any cost. How important is winning? Write a Response-to-Literature Essay addressing this subject.

11. Why didn't Patsy touch the trophy her team won? Write a story explaining how you think Patsy felt before she returned Tipper's trophy.

12. Ask students to design their own uniforms as described on page 73. They can design a team uniform for any league or team.

13. Jealousy is a problem for some of the characters in *The Basketball Mystery*. Lead a class discussion and list the instances of jealousy in the book. Ask students to mention how jealousy came between Buzz and Tipper, how it got Patsy to push for more attention from Tipper, and how Courtney and Frank acted toward the twins.

The Boxcar Children: The Basketball Mystery

It's a Girl's Game, Too

Less than a week after James Naismith invented his "Basket Ball" game, some women female school teachers happened to be going by the gym where the boys were playing and were impressed by the game. Naismith explained the rules, and they soon were playing.

Senda Berenson, a physical education instructor at Smith College, read about the new game in *The Triangle*, the student newspaper at Springfield, and set about devising her own rules to adapt the game for girls. She used three courts, instead of two, forbade players to leave their third of the court, introduced a rule to prevent any player from holding the ball over three seconds, and tried to tone down "masculine" behaviors such as snatching the ball or batting it away from another player. The game quickly became a hit at Smith College.

By 1895, the game had spread to New Orleans where Clara Gregory Baer renamed the game "Basquette" and adopted even more stringent and "ladylike" rules. Girls' basketball, under various rules, spread through the Midwest and on to California where the first intercollegiate games were played with scores as low as 2 to 1 and 6 to 5. Pomona College and Pasadena High School were early leaders in making the game popular.

Despite the best efforts of some basketball proponents to keep the game slow and gentle, the ladies' game was played with great vigor and enthusiasm. Bloomers were even reintroduced to make the players more comfortable. Games were often played outdoors on the grass.

By the 1920s, the game had become extremely popular, especially in such states as Texas, Oklahoma, and Iowa. Despite the opposition of some prominent women, including Margaret Mead and Lou Henry Hoover, the game remained popular. The fame of players like "Babe" Didrikson, the best woman athlete of her generation, helped reinforce a positive image of the game.

The women's game mirrored changes in the men's game as the peach basket was replaced by the open-ended net, the three-part court was reduced to the standard front court and back court, and the number of players was reduced to five.

Women basketball players were awarded the first full athletic scholarships in the early 1970s and the first NCAA women's tournament was held in 1982. Women's basketball became an Olympic sport in 1976. After several professional leagues had failed, the WNBA, formed in 1996, has been successful.

Some of the great women players of the past and present include Hazel Walker, Ann Myers, Nancy Lieberman, Lusia Harris, Molly Bolin, Cheryl Miller, Rebecca Lobo, Lisa Leslie, Chamique Holdsclaw, Cynthia Cooper, Lynette Woodward, and Sheryl Swoopes.

The Boxcar Children: The Basketball Mystery

Wheelchair Basketball

One of the reasons that basketball acquired so much popularity is that it is a very adaptable game. Even people with serious physical challenges are able to enjoy the game.

Wheelchair basketball was invented during World War II by disabled veterans. Wheelchair basketball is played by children and adults with a variety of physical problems, but nearly all of the players have lost the use of their legs.

Some players have back and stomach muscles which are paralyzed. They have to use their arms to keep from falling and to move the wheelchair. A second group have little or no use of their legs and feet. A third group are not paralyzed and have some control over their legs and feet but have one or both legs amputated.

Basketball wheelchairs are made of lighter materials than standard wheelchairs. They may cost $2,000 or more. They have hand rims, safety straps, and bicycle-sized wheels.

Some players dribble the ball with one hand and push the chair with the other hand. Other players have to hold the ball in their lap and push the chair twice. Then the player must bounce the ball off the floor.

Chair Shooting

You can get some sense of wheelchair basketball by playing this game. Tipper did a similar activity with the girls during the basketball clinic at the Aldens.

Directions

1. Divide your class into three teams. Use one chair and one ball for each team.
2. Place the three chairs near the center division line. Have one team member sit in the chair and have the remaining team line up behind their team chair. Use one half court for the teams.
3. One player on each team is the chair shooter. The chair shooter must remain in the chair and shoot from the chair. Dribbling is not necessary. The chair shooter may move but must remain seated, holding on to the seat of the chair and being careful not to block the other team's shooters.
4. The next player in each team's line retrieves missed balls. After the shooter has had three turns, he or she goes to the end of the line and the player retrieving the balls becomes the next shooter.
5. The team with the most number of baskets within a predetermined time is the winning team.

Hints for Chair Shooting

- Be sure the chair is directly facing the basket.
- Keep your back against the chair.
- Use a two-handed set shot when you first start.
- Push the ball away with both hands and arms until your elbows are fully extended.
- Pull your wrists down in your follow-through.

On the Court with . . . Michael Jordan

by Matt Christopher
(text by Glenn Stout)

Summary

On the Court with . . . Michael Jordan is an excellent account of the life of Michael Jordan from his early years in Brooklyn, New York, and Wilmington, North Carolina. His father's strong interest in sports and his parents concern that Michael study hard in school helped Michael keep his focus on being a hard worker both as an athlete and a student. As a boy, Michael found himself competing against his brothers and usually losing to his older and bigger siblings.

When Michael didn't make the cut for his high school team, he didn't quit. He just worked harder on his game as a junior varsity player and kept up his studies. He did make the team the following year and eventually became the star of the Laney High Buccaneers. So intensely serious about the game, he cut classes in order to practice, but his parents soon convinced him that he needed to balance his sports with his schoolwork.

On the Court with . . . Michael Jordan details Michael's success during the three years he played at the University of North Carolina and the difficulties he had in adjusting to the system and the discipline of college basketball. Michael's quandary about completing college or entering the NBA is explained and he did return to the University to complete his studies during the off season. Michael Jordan came out of college as one of the most heralded college players of his time but he didn't have instant success in the NBA. The author details the ups and downs Jordan encountered as a player supremely anxious to win a championship. Despite being chosen as Rookie of the Year in 1985, it would not be until 1991 when his team, the Chicago Bulls, finally became a championship team. In the course of those six years, Michael would not only refine his own game but also learn how to lead on the court and off. He would acquire the respect and the skill that would help make his teammates better players and his team a champion one.

The remaining chapters detail the Bulls' first three consecutive championships, the tragic death of his father, Michael's decision to play professional baseball, and his return to the NBA. It does not cover the final three championship years at the end of the 1990s.

This series of sports biographies is published under the Matt Christopher name and logo by Little, Brown and Company. They are written by various authors. Glenn Stout wrote the text of this Jordan biography.

On the Court with . . . Michael Jordan (cont.)

The outline below is a suggested plan for using the various activities and ideas that are presented in this unit. You should adapt these ideas to fit your own classroom situation.

Sample Lesson Plan

Day 1
- Conduct class discussion (Setting the Stage, #1, #2, #5).
- Read Chapters 1 and 2.
- Conduct SSR (Sustained Silent Reading).
- Discuss Michael Jordan's family and home life. What were his parents interested in? How did Michael get so involved with basketball? Why didn't Michael make his high school basketball team as a freshman? Why did he cut classes in high school? What question did his mom always ask when he called home from college? What decision did Michael have to make after three years in college?
- Do Nicknames page (Setting the Stage, #3).
- Discuss obstacles in life (Setting the Stage, #4).
- Start a reading journal.
- Write about declining interest in the NBA (Enjoying the Book, #2).
- Continue basketball skills.

Day 2
- Read Chapters 3 and 4.
- Conduct SSR.
- Discuss Michael Jordan's early career in the NBA. What problems did he have as a rookie? What awards did he receive? What goals did he fail to achieve? What happened to him at the All Star game?
- Continue the reading journal.
- Do Computing Points Per Game (Enjoying the Book, #3).
- Continue writing topic from Day 1.
- Continue basketball skills.

Day 3
- Read Chapters 5 and 6.
- Conduct SSR.
- Discuss Michael Jordan's role in the improvement of the Bulls. What did Michael have to learn to do in order to lead his team to a championship? What problems did he and the Bulls have to overcome?
- Continue the reading journal.
- Do Court Computations (Enjoying the Book, #4).
- Continue basketball skills.
- Discuss Career Guidance (Enjoying the Book, #6).

Day 4
- Read Chapters 7 and 8.
- Conduct SSR.
- Discuss Michael's troubles and successes as the Bulls win three straight championships. What errors in judgment did Michael make? Why did he want to win three straight championships?
- Continue the reading journal.
- Do Computing Shooting Percentage page (Enjoying the Book, #5).
- Introduce research project (Enjoying the Book, #7).

Day 5
- Read Chapters 9 through 11.
- Conduct SSR.
- Discuss the death of Michael's father. Why did Michael decide to play baseball? How good a baseball player was he? Why did he decide to return to basketball? What events have happened in Michael's life since this book was written?
- Conclude the reading journal.
- Read Michael Jordan: The Greatest Player Ever (Extending the Book, #1).
- Review Michael Jordan Time Line (Extending the Book, #2).
- Do Where the Pros Play (Extending the Book, #3).
- Do What's In a Name? (Extending the Book, #4).
- Continue the research project.
- Do Calculating Winning Percentages (Extending the Book, #7).
- Do Final Four Culminating Activity (Extending the Book, #10).

On the Court with...Michael Jordan

Overview of Activities

Setting the Stage

1. Ask students to name their favorite basketball player of all time. Lead the discussion into the attributes that determine a great player.

2. Lead a class discussion about Michael Jordan. Students should have a lot of prior knowledge about the man and his accomplishments.

3. Review **Nicknames** (page 18) with your students. Ask them to share their own nicknames and those of friends. Have students do the assignment at the top of the page.

4. Ask students to describe one obstacle they have had to overcome in life. It may have been difficulty learning times tables or learning to read, a serious illness or operation, the loss of a friend or parent or relative, or difficulty adjusting to a new school, a new home, or a new family.

5. Ask students what difficulties and problems Michael Jordan might have had as a player and student in school.

Enjoying the Book

1. Read the book *On the Court with . . . Michael Jordan* over the course of about five days. Your students should read about two chapters each day in SSR. Three chapters can be read on the last day.

2. Ask students to respond to this creative writing prompt:

   > In the last few years, attendance at NBA games has declined and so has the number of television viewers. What explanations could you give to account for this declining interest in the game? Be sure to consider player attitudes, the cost of attending games, competing activities, the quality of the games, and any other factors that you think might influence this decline.

3. Michael Jordan holds the record for the highest points per game in NBA history. This is the average number of points scored per games played. Have students complete **Computing Points Per Game** (page 49). Review the process of division if your students need it. Consider allowing students to use calculators to check their work after they have finished the computations with pencil and paper.

On the Court with...Michael Jordan

Overview of Activities *(cont.)*

Enjoying the Book *(cont.)*

4. Give a team of students the assignment of measuring the school basketball court dimensions with a yardstick. Instruct students to do **Court Computations** (page 50). Ask them to compare these measurements to the school courts.

5. Have students do **Computing Shooting Percentage** (page 52). Ask students to compute their own shooting percentages in classroom games or on their teams.

6. Michael Jordan developed his basketball career goals before high school. His parents always insisted that he get an education, too, and his mother always wanted to know his college grades first when he called home. Have students complete **Career Guidance** (page 15) to help them discern their own career goals based on their personal strengths and interests.

7. Have students research a famous basketball player. Discusss **Research the NBA Greats** (pages 62 and 63). Encourage students to become very familiar with the lives of their players. Encourage each student to select a different player. Ask students to give a brief oral presentation about their chosen player.

Extending the Book

1. Have students read **Michael Jordan: The Greatest Player Ever** (page 33). Ask them to carefully answer the comprehension questions (page 34). Instruct them to underline the part of the reading where each answer is found. (This is a good practice page for higher-level reading comprehension skills.)

2. Review the **Michael Jordan Time Line** (page 35) with students and have them complete the bottom part of the activity sheet. Encourage students to share the results of their research when they have finished. This time line can be done using the Internet, encyclopedias, and almanacs.

3. Michael Jordan has played in nearly every NBA arena. Review **Where the Pros Play** (page 56). Do the geography activity using the **U.S./Canada map** on page 57.

4. As a professional player, Michael Jordan played for the Chicago Bulls. Ask students how the Bulls might have received their name. Then have students do the activity **What's In a Name?** (page 58).

5. Have students complete **The College Game** (page 59), using the **U.S./Canada Map** (page 57). Ask students to use the page on **Olympic Basketball** (page 60) and the map (page 61) to record the listed nations that have Olympic basketball teams.

© Teacher Created Materials, Inc. 31 #3103 Thematic Unit—Basketball

Overview of Activities (cont.)

Extending the Book (cont.)

6. Have students design their own logos and posters (page 73) as an art activity. Encourage students to use community teams or local professional teams as their subjects. Display the posters and pennants on a bulletin board.

7. Use **Calculating Winning Percentages** (page 53) to teach students how to compute a team's winning percentage. If they play on a team, have students determine their own team's winning percentage.

8. Have students do the activity **Where the Money Is** (page 51). Review the process for subtracting large sums of money, if needed.

9. In the year 2001, George W. Bush was paid a $200,000 salary as President of the United States. Kevin Garnett made a salary that year of $19,610,000. Ask students to write a persuasive essay of at least three paragraphs expressing their opinion about the size of NBA salaries and the pay of other sports figures compared to people in other types of work. Stress that they offer at least three reasons in support of their position.

10. For the culminating activity in this thematic unit, organize a basketball theme day as described in **The Final Four** (page 74). Try to get some athletic parents or older students to referee the games and possibly conduct a clinic as Buzz and Tipper did in *The Boxcar Mystery*.

11. Be sure to award all participants a **Team Player Certificate** (page 77) and take plenty of pictures to display on a bulletin board. (See ideas on pages 75 and 76).

Michael Jordan: The Greatest Player Ever

Most sports fans can get into heated debates over who was the best player in a particular sport. Supporters of Babe Ruth or Henry Aaron or Willie Mays will argue endlessly over the best player in baseball history. Football and hockey fans can get just as intense in debating the merits of favorite players.

Basketball is different. Most fans of the game believe that Michael Jordan was the greatest player ever to play the game. They will admit that Wilt Chamberlain scored more points in his lifetime and that Shaquille O'Neal is an awesome center, but Michael Jordan did it all. His nickname was "Air Jordan" because he seemed to float forever through the air as he moved to the basket for a dunk or a finger roll. You only have to say "Michael" and everybody in basketball knows who you are talking about.

In his first year of college at North Carolina, he made the shot in the final game that won his team the national championship. In his next two years, he was named the best player in college basketball. In 1984, Michael was drafted by the Chicago Bulls, but knowing the value of education, he finished his college courses over the next two summers.

In the course of six NBA seasons, he went from being Rookie of the Year to becoming a celebrated basketball sensation on the court. He continued to refine his own skills, but it would not be until 1991 when the addition of outstanding players and his own maturity led to a Bulls' championship. For the next three years from 1991 to 1993, the Bulls would become the dominant team in the NBA and Jordan would be recognized as the best player in the league.

The murder of his father in 1993 had a profound effect on Michael Jordan. He felt that he needed to leave basketball. In 1993, Michael retired from the NBA to become a professional baseball player in the Chicago White Sox farm system which was owned by Jerry Reinsdorf, who also owned the Bulls. Michael played the 1994 baseball season for the Birmingham Barons and the Scottsdale Scorpions.

A combination of factors ended his baseball career. He was a pretty good outfielder but a poor hitter with little power. A baseball strike had crippled the game of baseball and Michael was unwilling to be a strikebreaker by becoming a baseball replacement player for the major leaguers. Finally, the lure of basketball was too great for Michael and in March of 1995, he returned to the Bulls. Although he led them into the playoffs that year, they were beaten in the second round by Orlando. In the following years, Jordan led the Bulls to three more consecutive championships before retiring again. In 2001, Michael again returned to the game to play for the Washington Wizards, a team which he partially owns.

On the Court with...Michael Jordan

Reading Comprehension Sheet

Directions: Carefully read the brief biography of Michael Jordan on the preceding page. Then circle the best answer for each question.

1. What is Michael Jordan's NBA nickname?
   A. Jord
   B. Iceman
   C. Air Jordan
   D. Bull

2. Where did Michael play his college basketball?
   A. North Dakota
   B. Northern California
   C. New York
   D. North Carolina

3. In what year did Michael Jordan play professional baseball?
   A. 1984
   B. 1993
   C. 1994
   D. 1996

4. Which baseball team was owned by Jerry Reinsdorf?
   A. Chicago Cubs
   B. Chicago White Sox
   C. Boston Red Sox
   D. New York Yankees

5. Which team is partially owned by Michael Jordan?
   A. Chicago Bulls
   B. Chicago White Sox
   C. Scottsdale Scorpions
   D. Washington Wizards

6. How many years did Michael Jordan play college basketball?
   A. 3
   B. 4
   C. 1
   D. 2

7. What happened to Michael's father in 1993?
   A. He bought the Bulls.
   B. He was murdered.
   C. He went to college.
   D. He got married.

8. What award did Jordan win in his first year in the NBA?
   A. Rookie of the Year
   B. MVP of the League
   C. Player of the Year
   D. College Player of the Year

9. In which three-year period did the Bulls first win three consecutive championships?
   A. 1994–1997
   B. 1991–1993
   C. 1996–1999
   D. 1984–1987

10. Which phrase best describes Michael Jordan's baseball skills?
    A. great hitter, poor fielder
    B. pretty good fielder, poor hitter
    C. great fielder, power hitter
    D. poor fielder, power hitter

On the Court with...Michael Jordan

Time Line: Michael Jordan and the United States

1963   Michael Jordan is born on Feb. 17 in Brooklyn, New York.
1970   The Jordan family moves to Wilmington, North Carolina.
1977   Michael doesn't make his high school basketball team.
1981   Michael graduates from Laney High School.
1982   Michael makes the final shot leading North Carolina to the NCAA national championship.
1984   Michael is drafted by the NBA's Chicago Bulls.
1985   Michael is named NBA Rookie of the Year.
1986   Michael scores an NBA record of 63 points in a playoff game.
1988   Jordan is named the NBA's Most Valuable Player.
1989   Michael marries Juanita Vanoy.
1991   Michael leads the Bulls to NBA championship.
1993   Michael leads the Bulls to its third consecutive national title and retires from basketball.
1994   Michael plays baseball for the Chicago White Sox farm system.
1995   Michael returns to the Bulls.
1996   Michael leads the Bulls to another NBA title.
1998   Michael and the Bulls win their sixth NBA title in the 1990s.

Directions: Study the important dates in Michael Jordan's life above. Then use almanacs, history books, encyclopedias, the Internet, and other resources to find one thing that happened in United States history during that same year. Record the events on the second time line below.

1963 _____
1970 _____
1977 _____
1981 _____
1982 _____
1984 _____
1985 _____
1986 _____
1988 _____
1989 _____
1991 _____
1993 _____
1994 _____
1995 _____
1996 _____
1998 _____

Literature

Matt Christopher: Sports Author

Matt Christopher played baseball, basketball, soccer, and football as a child . . . and he read every book he could find in the library. Both his love of sports and his love for books led him to a career as a writer.

Matthew Christopher was born on August 16, 1917, in Bath, Pennsylvania, to immigrant parents who neither read nor wrote English. His mother was Hungarian and his father was Italian. He was the oldest of nine children. Although his family was poor, Matt seemed to have had an enjoyable childhood growing up in a community with friends of many nationalities and backgrounds. Although Matt decided to become a writer when he was 14, it was many years before he could make writing a career. He was too poor to afford a college education and was also weak in mathematics but he was skilled in writing poetry, songs, and essays and was encouraged by a teacher, his coach, and his principal to use his talents. As a young man he worked as a day laborer, a minor-league baseball player, and a factory worker. Later, he held jobs as a member of the production staff for National Cash Register and a technical editor.

Matt Christopher's first book, published in 1952, was an adult mystery. His first children's story was *The Lucky Baseball Bat* published in 1954. These were followed by *Baseball Pals* in 1956 and *Basketball Sparkplug* in 1957. In 1963, after writing 12 books in 10 years, Mr. Christopher decided to quit his job and devote all of his time to writing.

Mr. Christopher's books reflect many of his early experiences as an athlete in school and as a minor-league baseball player. His books often deal with themes that are especially important today, such as being a member of a minority group on a team that is unwilling to accept a player because of his race and about child athletes who suffer from a disability, such as diabetes or stuttering. The themes of acceptance, earning the respect of teammates, and triumphing over all obstacles are characteristic of most of his books.

Matt Christopher's writing style is simple, easy to understand, and strong on realistic dialogue between children. He is particularly skilled in describing the action of a game or athletic event. Children find that the stories are filled with a good deal of sports action and they can understand the subtle themes in the writing.

Matt Christopher died on September 20, 1997, from a brain tumor, a condition he fought for the last 12 years of his life.

About the Author: Gertrude Chandler Warner

Gertrude Chandler Warner was born in Putnam, Connecticut in 1890. From their earliest school years, Gertrude and her sister were intensely interested in writing. In 1918, at the age of 28, Gertrude became a grade school teacher in Putnam, a job she would hold for 32 years despite a variety of illnesses and injuries.

Gertrude began writing professionally for children shortly after beginning her teaching career and published a variety of books and stories for children over the course of her lifetime. She originally wrote *The Boxcar Children* during an illness when she couldn't teach school. She based the story on her own youthful desire to live in a boxcar, to hang her wash out in a little back yard, and to cook in the freight car on a rusty old stove found in an abandoned caboose.

The original *Boxcar Children* was written and published in 1924 by Rand McNally. In 1942, she was asked to revise *The Boxcar Children* and use a controlled vocabulary of 600 words in a 15,000-word book. This book was used as a school reader for young children and as a remedial book for teenagers.

Gertrude Chandler Warner often included her own interests in her writing. Her fondness for butterflies and other insects, birds, flowers, gardens, rocks, woods, and other wonders of nature are often reflected in the interests of one or another of the Boxcar Children. Her love of books, reading, and learning are clearly expressed in each book in some way.

Unlike most modern writers, she wrote her books first in pen in 100-page notebooks before typing them for submission to the publisher. She published the further adventures of the Boxcar Children in *Surprise Island* in 1949 and *The Yellow House Mystery* in 1953. She continued the mystery series into the 1970s.

Gertrude Warner also wrote a variety of other less successful children's books, including a retelling of the *Arabian Nights Star Stories*, *The World on a Farm*, and *Windows into Alaska*. She also co-authored some adult books with her sister and wrote a *History of Connecticut*.

In another area of her life, Gertrude was very active in the American Red Cross. She continued this service for over 50 years.

Gertrude Chandler Warner died August 30, 1979, in Putnam. Her publisher, Albert Whitman & Company, has continued the Boxcar series with other authors who remain true to the original themes and characters of the series, but with settings and plots set in the present.

Literature

Meet the Boxcar Children

You won't want to read just one of the Boxcar mysteries. After reading *The Boxcar Children: The Basketball Mystery*, you may find yourself wanting to read more. The original story, *The Boxcar Children*, is as exciting and intriguing today as it was when it was released more than sixty years ago.

In the original story, we first meet four hungry and orphaned children standing in front of a bakery. The oldest is Henry, who is about 12, and the youngest is Benny, who is about 5. Violet is about 10 and Jessie is slightly older. They enter the bakery and buy three loaves of bread.

The baker's wife allows the orphans to sleep in the shop at night but she does not like children, especially boys. They overhear her telling the baker that she would keep the three older children to work for them but that the youngest, Benny, must go to a local orphanage.

The children quietly leave in the dark of the night and quickly move out of town. They have already walked a long way since their parents died. They know they have a grandfather somewhere but they believe he doesn't like them because he didn't like their mother. They sleep during the day and walk at night until good fortune brings them to a deserted boxcar sitting near a river.

The children set up housekeeping in the old railroad car while Henry goes to a nearby town and finds work helping a doctor and his mother with chores. All of the children demonstrate self-reliance and resourcefulness in making do with what they have. Jessie helps turn the boxcar into a home and the near-by stream becomes their pool and bathtub. They acquire a stray dog they call Watch. The children build an outdoor fireplace. They find wild plants to eat along with food that Henry brings from town. Jessie even starts teaching Benny to read.

The children are quite happily settled into their new life when several events occur. Henry enters a race in a local fair and wins. The wealthy man who organizes this annual event, James Henry Aleden, awards him the twenty-five-dollar prize. The doctor Henry works for sees a notice posted by this same wealthy man and reads that he is looking for four lost grandchildren. Finally, Violet gets very sick and Henry asks the doctor for help.

Every reader will enjoy the conclusion of this book and look forward to reading more in the series. The four Boxcar Children show curiosity and courage, and common sense and hard work in taking care of each other and helping others. They are great people to meet in the pages of these books.

Drama and Poetry

Readers' Theater

Readers' Theater is drama without costumes, props, stage, or memorization. It is done in the classroom by groups of students who become the cast of the dramatic reading.

Staging

Your classroom is the stage. Place four or five stools in a semicircle at the front of your class or in a separate staging area. If you have no stools, have students sit on the tops of desks, facing the audience. Students may use simple costumes like hats or coats, but generally no costume is expected or used in this type of dramatization.

If you have plain robes or simple coats of the same color or style so that everyone looks about the same, this can have a nice effect. Students dressed in the same school uniform or colors create an atmosphere of seriousness. Props are not needed, but they may be used for additional details.

Scripting

Readers' Theater can be done using a standard play format. It is also easy to convert well-written dialogue from children's literature into a dramatic format.

Keep the number of actors to four or five at most. The most important reader with the largest amount of text is the narrator. You can easily have the narrator role divided between two actors, if the text is long.

If you pick a children's book, such as *Center Court Sting* or *The Boxcar Children*, find a selection with a good deal of exciting or interesting dialogue.

- Assign the narrator to the sections without quotes.
- Assign separate actors to each role in the dialogue, such as Daren, Lou, Coach Michaels, Jessie, Buzz, or Tipper. If there are too many roles, have one actor do two parts. (Make sure these two parts don't have to talk to each other.)
- Drop the inter-dialogue remarks such as "he said," "answered Buzz," or "Lou insisted."
- Copy the text so that each child has a clearly marked, useable script.
- Place scripts in folders that are uniform in color and size.
- Allow children to practice several times over several days before presenting in front of the class.

Performing

Students should enter quietly and seriously into a dimly lit room, with the scripts held in the same position. Actors should sit silently and unmoving on the stools or desks and wait with head lowered or alternatively focusing on a point above the audience such as a clock. The narrator should start reading and the actors will then focus on their scripts. The actors should focus on whoever is reading, except when they are performing.

Extensions

Encourage students to add movement and memorization to performances after they have had several experiences in Readers' Theater. They can introduce mime to the performance and add props or costumes, as the circumstances allow. Some students may begin to add accents as they become more familiar with the drama.

© Teacher Created Materials, Inc.

Drama and Poetry

Readers' Theater *(cont.)*

Readers' Theater Activities

1. Convert one of these sections from *Center Court Sting* (The version used here was published in 1998 by Little, Brown, and Company) to a script for Readers' Theater.
2. Practice reading the scripts with the group for several days.
3. Present the Readers' Theater to your class audience.

Selection Choices from *Center Court Sting*

Pages 1 through 5

Dialogue and gestures between Daren, the ref, and Coach Michaels
- Use four actors: Narrator, Daren, Ref, and Coach.
- Write a brief narrator's introduction for pages 1 and 2.

Pages 9 through 15

Dialogue in the clubhouse and on the bus after the game
- Use six actors: Daren, Coach, Andy, Lou, Shawn, and Lynn.
- Write a brief introduction to the scene for the Narrator.

Pages 16 through 18

Dialogue between Daren and his friend, Lynn
- Use three actors: Narrator, Daren, and Lynn.
- Write a brief introduction to the scene for the Narrator.

From the bottom of page 23 to the middle of page 26
- Use five actors: Narrator, Daren, Lynn, Lou, and Shawn.
- Write a brief introduction to the scene for the Narrator.

From the middle of page 38 to page 45
- Use five actors: Narrator, Daren, Lynn, Gary, and Judy.
- Write a brief introduction to the scene for the Narrator.

From the middle of page 60 to page 65
- Use five actors—some will do two parts: Narrator, Daren, Lynn, Lou, Shawn, Peter, Cris, Coach, other players
- Write a brief introduction to the scene for the Narrator.

From the bottom of page 65 through page 69
- Use three actors: Narrator, Daren, and Lou.
- Write a brief introduction to the scene for the Narrator.

Chapter 9
- Use four actors: Narrator, Lynn, Daren, and Judy.
- Write a brief introduction to the scene and description of the meeting with Judy and Gary for the Narrator.

Pages 76 through 81
- Use three actors: Narrator, Daren, and Dad.
- Write a brief introduction to the scene for the Narrator.

Readers' Theater (cont.)

Converting Stories to Drama

You can write and perform your own Readers' Theater scripts using the following suggestions:

- Watch two really good players in your class go one-on-one against each other for a few minutes or observe a good game of basketball at school during recess or P.E. You could also watch a few minutes of a televised college or NBA game.
- Take notes of the action that occurs. Be sure to mention who's shooting and from where, any fouls that occur, and every exciting or interesting move. If the real game is not exciting enough, create an imaginary game with real or imaginary players. Be sure to fill the story with plenty of action and to make the game tight and exciting. Use **Basketball Terms** (page 47) and **Basketball Lingo** (page 48).
- Convert this creative writing activity to a script with two announcers. You may adopt the names of real announcers or make up your own names, clubs, television or radio station, players, and basketball arenas. Feel free to add commercials and interviews with players and fans.
- You will need two main readers for the announcers and one or two other readers for the fans, players, commercials, and other commentary. You might want to add props, such as fake microphones, or add sounds to heighten the realism of the game.

Converting Other Books

Choose a chapter, with several characters and a lot of dialogue, from one of your favorite books. Use a narrator for the basic introduction and text and different readers to do the dialogue. Remember to drop the "he saids" and other unimportant words.

The following books work well for this project:

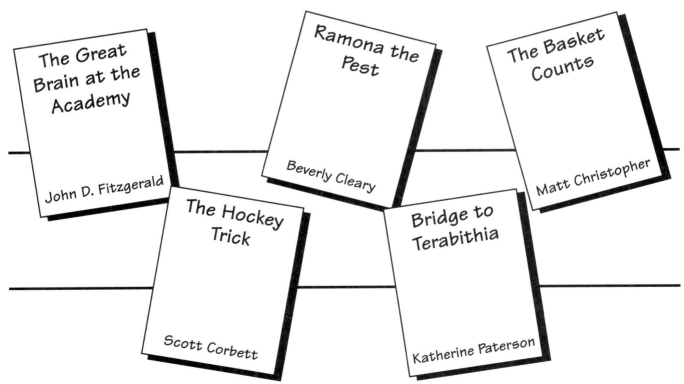

- The Great Brain at the Academy — John D. Fitzgerald
- Ramona the Pest — Beverly Cleary
- The Basket Counts — Matt Christopher
- The Hockey Trick — Scott Corbett
- Bridge to Terabithia — Katherine Paterson

Drama and Poetry

The Poetry of Basketball

Sometimes a poem says it best. Read the poem "Foul Shot" by Edwin A. Hoey. This poem and others like it can set the scene.

You can find the poem and learn whether the player made the basket or not in a poetry collection called *Opening Days/Sports Poems* selected by Lee Bennett Hopkins. The illustrations are excellent and the poems share insights into other sports, as well.

Poetry in Two Voices

An effective way to make poetry dynamic is to encourage two children to recite the poem together. They may recite alternate verses for part of the poem and recite some sections together as a choral reading. This technique can be used with any of the sports poems from *Opening Days* or other children's poems such as the color poems from *Hailstones and Halibut Bones*. For poems that are written to be read in two voices, try Paul Fleishman's Newbery Award winning *Joyful Noise*, a collection of poems about insects.

Poetry in Two Voices

Directions

1. Choose a partner.

2. Choose a poem from the collection your teacher has provided. Pick a poem that appeals to you because of the rhythm or subject matter.

3. Divide up the poem into parts so that you and your partner can recite the poem back and forth. Practice reciting together so that you have the same speed, volume, and pace.

4. Recite the poem for the class.

Student Partners: _____

Poem Chosen: _____

We will practice and recite our poem on _____

                                                                   (date)

Signature: _____

Drama and Poetry

Write Your Own Poetry

Cinquains

Cinquains are five-line poems that follow the following specific pattern. They are usually arranged in the shape shown below.

Pattern

Line 1—one word *(noun or title of the poem)*

Line 2—two words *(adjectives, description)*

Line 3—three words *(verbs; action words ending in either -ing or -ed but not both)*

Line 4—four words *(usually a phrase expressing feeling)*

Line 5—one word *(summation; usually a noun or synonym for title)*

Directions: Study the example below. Then write your own cinquain on the lines provided. Consider using basketball or another favorite sport as the subject. (The most formal cinquain follows a syllable pattern of 2-4-6-8-2 for the five lines. Check to see if your poem matches this pattern.)

Example

Basketball
Fierce, focused
Dribbling, driving, shooting
It requires intense discipline
Hoops

_____

_____ _____

_____ _____ _____

_____ _____ _____ _____

_____

© Teacher Created Materials, Inc.   43   #3103 Thematic Unit—Basketball

Drama and Poetry

Write Your Own Poetry (cont.)

Directions: Study the examples below. Then write your own diamante poems on another sheet of paper. Consider using basketball or another favorite sport as the subject of one of your poems.

Diamante

Diamante poems are seven-line poems that form a specific pattern. They are usually arranged in the diamond shape shown below.

Pattern One

Line 1—one word *(noun-title or subject of the poem)*

Line 2—two words *(adjectives, description)*

Line 3—three words *(verbs; action words ending in either **ing** or **ed** but not both)*

Line 4—four words *(nouns related to the subject)*

Line 5—three words *(verbs, action words ending in either **ing** or **ed** but not both)*

Line 6—two words *(adjectives, description)*

Line 7—one word *(summation—noun or synonym for title)*

Player
Smooth, relaxed
Dribbling, driving, jumping, scoring
Lay-up, jumper, hook, dunk
Leaping, grabbing, passing, slamming
Agile, artistic
Shooter

Pattern Two

A more complex form of the poem uses an antonym in line seven for the subject. The last two nouns in line four and the words in lines five and six refer to the contrasting noun in line seven.

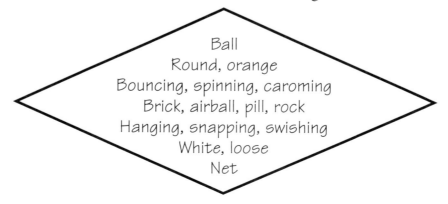

Ball
Round, orange
Bouncing, spinning, caroming
Brick, airball, pill, rock
Hanging, snapping, swishing
White, loose
Net

Write Your Own Poetry (cont.)

I like . . .

The formula for this type of poetry is to add a descriptive word to each line, making the final line the summation. These poems can help develop descriptive vocabulary and rhyme.

Example

I like hoops.
I like slick hoops.
I like smooth, slick hoops.
I like smooth, slick hoops with dunks.
I like smooth, slick hoops with slamming dunks.
I like smooth, slick hoops with slamming, jamming dunks.
I like smooth, slick hoops with slamming, jamming dunks over friends.

Directions: Write two I like . . . poems about basketball, another sport, or a topic of your choice.

I like _____.

I like _____ _____.

I like _____ _____ _____.

I like _____ _____ _____ _____.

I like _____ _____ _____ _____ _____.

I like _____ _____ _____ _____ _____ _____.

I like _____ _____ _____ _____ _____ _____ _____.

I like _____.

I like _____ _____.

I like _____ _____ _____.

I like _____ _____ _____ _____.

I like _____ _____ _____ _____ _____.

I like _____ _____ _____ _____ _____ _____.

I like _____ _____ _____ _____ _____ _____ _____.

Drama and Poetry

Write Your Own Poetry (cont.)

I wish . . .

The formula for this type of poetry is to write a wish on the first line. The rest of the poem is based on the wish. This type of poem has a very flexible format.

I wish I was a basketball star.

I'd move like greased lightning

With slippery, slickery speed,

And sudden spurts and dashes,

Driving fiercely through the lane.

No opponent could stop me.

I'd slamma-jamma the ball

So hard the net would singe

While the glass board shuddered.

Fans would scream to the rafters

While foes clenched their jaws

And talked wildly to themselves.

I wish I was the next Michael.

Directions: On another sheet of paper, write your own "I wish . . ." poem. Use a basketball or sports topic or choose something else you especially like.

Language Arts

Basketball Terms

Directions: On another sheet of paper, use the following terms to describe the action in a play-by-play account of one period in a basketball game. Try to use 15 terms.

assist	a pass from a teammate that leads directly to a basket
bounce pass	a pass from one player to another by bouncing the ball on the floor
cut	a quick move by an offensive player toward the basket
dribble	a player bounces the ball with the ball held palm down
double dribble	a player dribbles the ball, stops, and then dribbles again
double team	two defensive players guard one offensive player
fast break	a player gets the ball at the defensive end of the court and throws the ball to a teammate breaking toward the basket for a lay-up
field goal	a shot worth either two or three points
foul	a violation of the rules in which a player is hit or pushed
free throw	a foul shot worth one point taken from a line 15 feet from the basket
full-court press	a defensive technique used by a team over the entire court to disrupt an offense
high post	a position played by the center on offense near the top of the free throw circle
lay-up	a drive toward the basket with a shot taken close to the basket
low post	a position played by the center on offense near the basket
paint	the painted area between the foul line and the out-of-bounds line under the basket; often called the key or the lane
rebound	a ball that has bounced off the backboard or rim into a player's possession
screen	a play in which an offensive player blocks out a defensive player so his teammate can take a shot
shot clock	a 24-second clock used to time possession of the ball until a shot is made or attempted
three (3)	a field goal worth three points shot beyond an arc 22 feet from the basket
traveling	a violation in which a player takes too many steps without dribbling the ball
turnover	losing the ball to the other team from a bad pass, a lost dribble, a stolen ball, or an offensive foul
transition	the time when the ball changes hands from one team to the other after a score or an attempted score
zone defense	a defensive technique in which a defender guards a part of the court rather than one player

© Teacher Created Materials, Inc.   #3103 Thematic Unit—Basketball

Language Arts

Basketball Lingo

Directions: Read the following figurative expressions and their meanings. Then use some of them in your poetry writing or choose some of them to illustrate (cartoons work best) on another sheet of paper. For example, for aircraft carrier, you could draw a basketball player who looks like a huge plane wearing a uniform and bouncing a basketball on the court.

air ball	a shot that misses so badly it doesn't even touch the rim
aircraft carrier	a nickname for a big center who dominates the space under the basket
alley-oop	a pass thrown to a player who leaps up, catches the pass, and usually dunks the ball
boxing out	a player keeps his body between the basket and a player on the other team to be in a better position to get a rebound
brick	a hard shot that ricochets off the rim or board
bunny	an easy, open shot
bury	to hit a long shot
coast-to-coast	to take the ball from one end of the court to a lay-up at the other basket
give-and-go	one player passes to a teammate, breaks to the basket, and then the teammate passes the ball back to him
glory-hunter	a player who is more concerned with his points than the team's performance
gunner	a player who shoots the ball a lot, often without setting up a good play
hook shot	a one-handed sweeping shot taken over the shooter's head
J	a jump shot
NBN	a shot so smooth it hits *nothing but net*
palming	an illegal dribble in which a player holds his palm under the ball and then bounces it
pill	the ball
rejection	a blocked shot
rock	a poor shot that caroms hard off the rim or board
slam-dunk	a shot thrown downward through the basket by a player with excellent leaping ability
skyhook	a hook shot taken when the shooter's hand is at the top of the arc
skywalk	the ability to change directions while in the air
360	a complete, 360-degree turn designed to elude a defender
triple double	an unusual accomplishment in a game where one player has 10 or more in three of these categories: points, assists, rebounds, steals, and blocked shots

Computing Points per Game

One of the statistics used to compare great players is "points per game" which means the average number of points a player scored in all the games he played in a year or a career.

You can compute the PPG (points per game) of a player this way:

1. Determine the total points scored by a player in a season or a career.
2. Determine the number of games an individual played.
3. Divide the total number of points by the total number of games played.

Grant Hill

Total games: 439

Total points: 9,448

```
            21.5
      _____
439 ) 9448.0
      - 878
      -----
        668
      - 439
      -----
        229 0
      - 219 5
      -------
          9 5
```

Round the answer to one decimal **Points per game: 21.5**

Directions: Compute the career PPG (points per game) for each player listed below. Then use the chart to answer the following questions.

Player	Total Games	Total Points	Points per Game (PPG)
Larry Bird	897	21,791	
Elgin Baylor	846	23,149	
Karl Malone	1,273	32,919	
Hakeem Olajuwon	1,177	26,511	
Patrick Ewing	1,118	24,425	
Wilt Chamberlain	1,045	31,419	
Michael Jordan	930	29,277	
Julius Erving	836	18,364	
Oscar Robertson	1,040	26,710	
Kareem Abdul-Jabbar	1,560	38,387	
Shaquille O'Neal	608	16,812	
Jerry West	932	25,192	
Pete Maravich	658	15,948	
David Thompson	509	11,264	
Charles Barkley	1,073	23,757	

1. Which player had the highest PPG? _____
2. Which of the above players played in the most games? _____
3. Which player had the most points scored? _____

Math

Court Computations

NBA Court Dimensions

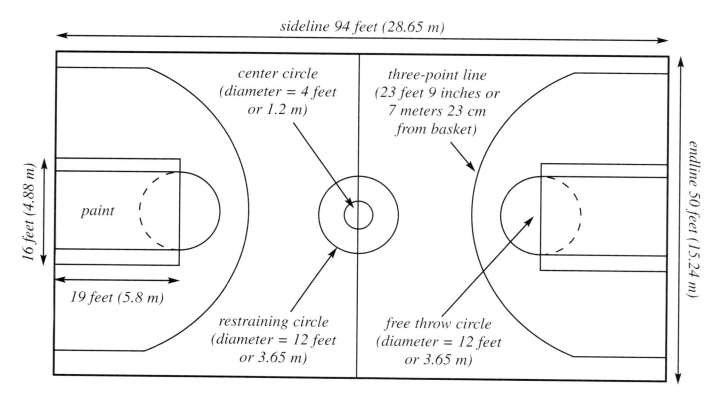

Directions: Use the information on this page and the formulas below to answer the questions.

Formulas: area of a rectangle = length x width   area of a circle = radius² x 3.14
circumference = diameter x 3.14   radius = ½ x diameter

1. What is the perimeter of the NBA court? _____

2. What is the area of the basketball court? _____

3. What is the perimeter of the paint? _____

4. What is the area of the paint? _____

5. What is the circumference of the free throw circle? _____

6. What is the circumference of the center circle? _____

7. What is the area of the free throw circle? _____

8. What is the area of the center circle? _____

Math

Where the Money Is

More than 63 players in the NBA made at least $7,000,000 a year at the beginning of 2001. Below is a list of some top NBA salaries according to some published reports. These salaries may change over time.

Player	Salary
Kevin Garnett	$19,610,000
Shaquille O'Neal	$19,285,715
Juwan Howard	$16,900,000
Alonzo Mourning	$16,880,000
Hakeem Olajuwon	$16,700,000
Karl Malone	$15,750,000
Scottie Pippen	$13,750,000
Gary Payton	$12,200,000
John Stockton	$11,000,000
Reggie Miller	$10,670,000
Kobe Bryant	$10,130,000
Allen Iverson	$10,130,000
Grant Hill	$ 9,660,000
Jason Kidd	$ 7,680,000

Directions: Use the chart above to answer these questions.

1. Who is the highest paid player listed? _____
2. How much more was Kevin Garnett paid than Shaquille O'Neal? _____
3. How much more money did Karl Malone earn than his teammate John Stockton? _____
4. How much do Kobe Bryant and Shaquille O'Neal's combined salaries total? _____
5. How much money did the top five players on the list earn all together? _____
6. How much less money did Grant Hill make than Gary Payton? _____
7. Who earned more—Allen Iverson or Kobe Bryant? _____
8. How much money did all of the players make together? _____
9. What was the average earnings of the 14 players on the chart? (Compute average by adding all salaries and dividing by 14.) _____
10. Which player's salary was closest to the average salary? _____

Math

Computing Shooting Percentages

- To compute shooting percentage, divide the number of shots made by the number of shots attempted.
- Shooting percentages can be calculated to two places and written as percent.
- Field goals, three-point field goals, and free throws are computed in the same way.

Example

Kobe Bryant attempted 1,510 field goals in the 2000–2001 season. He made 701 field goals. What was his shooting percentage?

Divide. $1510\overline{)701}$ *Add three zeros.*

```
           .464
1510 ) 701.000
      -604 0
        97 00
       -90 60
        6 400
       -6 040
          360
```

Round to two places. **Kobe Bryant's shooting percentage is 46%.**

Directions: Compute these shooting percentages.

1. Gary Payton took 272 three-point shots and made 102 of them. What was his shooting percentage? _____

2. Rick Fox took 300 three-point field goals and made 118 shots. What was his shooting percentage? _____

3. John Stockton attempted 651 field goals in the 2000–2001 season. He made 328 shots. What was his shooting percentage? _____

4. Shaquille O'Neal attempted 1,422 field goals in the 2000–2001 season. He made 813 field goals. What was his shooting percentage? _____

5. David Robinson made 400 field goals out of 823 attempts. What was his shooting percentage?
_____

6. Vince Carter made 162 three-pointers out of 397 attempts. What was his shooting percentage?
_____

7. John Stockton attempted 132 three-point shots and made 61 in the 2000–2001 season. What was his shooting percentage? _____

8. Kevin Garnett made 704 field goals in 1,457 attempts. What was his shooting percentage?
_____

Calculating Winning Percentages

- You can calculate a team's winning percentage by dividing the number of games won by the number of games played.
- Winning percentages are calculated to three decimal places and written as a decimal—like batting averages.

Example

Miami won 50 out of 82 games in the 2000–2001 season.

Divide. $82\overline{)50}$ Add a decimal and four zeros.

```
      .6097
82) 50.0000
   -49 2
      8000
    - 738
       620
     - 574
        46
```

Round the answer to three decimal points. **Miami's winning percentage is .610.**

Directions: Compute the winning percentages of these teams for the year 2000–2001.

	Team	Won	Lost	Played	Winning Percentage
1.	Philadelphia	56	26	82	
2.	New York	48	34	82	
3.	L.A. Lakers	56	26	82	
4.	Chicago	15	67	82	
5.	Indiana	41	41	82	
6.	Portland	50	32	82	
7.	Utah	53	29	82	
8.	Denver	40	42	82	
9.	Sacramento	55	27	82	
10.	Dallas	53	29	82	
11.	Atlanta	25	57	82	
12.	Toronto	47	35	82	
13.	L.A. Clippers	31	51	82	
14.	Boston	36	46	82	
15.	San Antonio	58	24	82	
16.	Golden State	17	65	82	

1. Which team had the highest winning percentage? _____
2. Which team had a .500 winning percentage? _____
3. Which teams had identical winning percentages? _____

Social Studies/Geography

Basketball Chronology

Directions

1. Read the following two-page chronology of some of the great events in basketball history.
2. Find at least 20 events in United States or world history that occurred on the dates listed below. For example, Thomas Edison invented the motion picture camera in 1891, the same year that basketball was invented.

Helpful Hints

- Use encyclopedias, almanacs, basketball books, history texts, the Internet, and other sources.
- The events may include wars, years a president was in office, and events such as the first man to walk on the moon.
- If you know of an important date in history, try to find other important events in basketball history that happened at the same time.

Basketball Chronology

1891 In December, Dr. James Naismith introduced his newly invented game of "Basket Ball" to his physical education class in Springfield, Massachusetts.

1892 The first public basketball game was held in March between students and teachers at the Springfield Christian Association School.

Senda Berenson, a physical education teacher at Smith College, adapted Dr. Naismith's rules to create a woman's version of the game.

1893 Metal hoops with net bags replaced wooden peach baskets. A cord was pulled to release the ball.

Students of both genders played intramural basketball at Iowa State College.

1894 Backboards were introduced to protect spectators.

Larger balls were used instead of soccer balls.

Free throws were shot from 15 feet.

1895 Field goals were worth 2 points; free throws were worth 1 point.

1896 The University of Chicago beat the University of Iowa in the first men's college game.

The Stanford ladies defeated the University of California in the first women's college game.

1897 Teams were limited to five players on the floor.

1901 The Ivy League became the first league with organized college basketball games.

1913 Nets without a bottom were used.

1927 The Harlem Globetrotters were organized and began touring the nation.

1929 The cage—a court surrounded by rope or chicken wire to protect the spectators—was eliminated.

1932 Courts are divided into a front court and a back court. The 10-second rule requiring the offense to move the ball over the center line was adopted.

1935 Time in the lane was limited to 3 seconds.

1936 Men's basketball became an Olympic sport.

Social Studies/Geography

Basketball Chronology (cont.)

1937 The jump ball after each basket was eliminated.

The first national college tournament, the NIT, was played.

1939 The first NCAA national tournament was played.

Dr. Naismith, the game's founder, died.

1949 The NBA was formed.

1950 Chuck Cooper and Earl Lloyd became the first African-American players in the NBA.

1954 The 24-second shot clock was introduced in the NBA.

1959 The Basketball Hall of Fame was established.

The Boston Celtics won the first of eight straight NBA championships.

1960 Philadelphia's Wilt Chamberlain grabbed 55 rebounds in one game.

1962 Wilt Chamberlain scored 100 points in one game.

1964 The NBA foul lane was widened to 16 feet.

1966 The Boston Celtics won their eighth straight championship.

Bill Russell became the first African-American NBA coach.

1967 The American Basketball Association was formed to compete with the NBA.

1968 The Basketball Hall of Fame opened in Springfield, Massachusetts.

1972 The Los Angeles Lakers won 33 consecutive games.

1973 Ann Myers became the first woman to receive a full basketball scholarship to UCLA.

1976 The ABA went out of business after nine years.

The NBA expanded to 22 teams.

Women's basketball became an Olympic event.

1977 The Women's Basketball Association was started and lasted three years.

1979 The NBA adopted the three-point field goal.

Magic Johnson and the Michigan Spartans defeated Larry Bird and the Indiana State Sycamores, a game that popularized the NCAA tournament.

1982 The first NCAA women's tournament was held.

1985 Lynette Woodward became the first woman Globetrotter.

1992 The Dream Team won the Olympic gold medal.

The first two women were inducted into the Basketball Hall of Fame.

1993 Michael Jordan retires.

1996 The Chicago Bulls had the best win-loss record of all time with a 72-10 season.

1997 The WNBA began playing. It currently has 16 teams.

1998 The Chicago Bulls won their third consecutive NBA title.

Michael Jordan retired again.

2001 The Los Angeles Lakers with Kobe Bryant and Shaquille O'Neal won their second NBA title in a row.

Social Studies/Geography

Where the Pros Play

Below is a list of the 29 NBA teams.

Directions: Label each team on the U.S./Canada map on the next page. Then answer the questions at the bottom of the page. Please note that the information here was correct at the time this book was published. Sometimes teams change locations.

NBA Teams

Atlanta Hawks	Milwaukee Bucks
Boston Celtics	Minnesota Timberwolves
Charlotte Hornets	New Jersey Nets
Chicago Bulls	New York Knicks
Cleveland Cavaliers	Orlando Magic
Dallas Mavericks	Philadelphia 76ers
Denver Nuggets	Phoenix Suns
Detroit Pistons	Portland Trail Blazers
Golden State Warriors	Sacramento Kings
Houston Rockets	San Antonio Spurs
Indiana Pacers	Seattle SuperSonics
Los Angeles Clippers	Toronto Raptors
Los Angeles Lakers	Utah Jazz
Memphis Grizzlies	Washington Wizards
Miami Heat	

NBA Questions

1. How many states in the United States have an NBA team? _____
2. How many NBA teams play in Canada? _____
3. How many NBA teams are located in cities west of the Mississippi River? _____
4. How many NBA teams are located in cities east of the Mississippi River? _____
5. Which state has the most NBA teams? _____
6. How many states have no NBA teams? _____
7. How many NBA teams play in California? _____
8. How many NBA teams play in Texas? _____

Social Studies/Geography

What's in a Name?

Directions: Use a dictionary and your imagination to suggest the meaning of each team's name. Write why you think each club chose the name it did.

Hawks _____

Celtics _____

Hornets _____

Bulls _____

Cavaliers _____

Mavericks _____

Nuggets _____

Pistons _____

Golden State Warriors _____

Rockets _____

Pacers _____

Clippers _____

Lakers _____

Heat _____

Bucks _____

Timberwolves _____

Nets _____

Knicks _____

Magic _____

76ers _____

Suns _____

Trail Blazers _____

Kings _____

Spurs _____

SuperSonics _____

Jazz _____

Grizzlies _____

Wizards _____

Raptors _____

Social Studies/Geography

The College Game

Basketball quickly became a popular game on American college campuses. Colleges soon had intramural teams and later developed men's and women's teams which competed in conferences.

Directions: Listed below are some of the great college and university teams in the United States. Write each college in the correct state on the U.S./Canada map on page 57.

College/University	Location (City/State)
Duke	Durham, NC
UCLA	Los Angeles, CA
Kentucky	Lexington, KY
North Carolina	Chapel Hill, NC
Tennessee	Knoxville, TN
Arkansas	Fayetteville, AR
Syracuse	Syracuse, NY
UNLV	Las Vegas, NV
St. John's	Jamaica, NY
Utah	Salt Lake City, UT
Indiana	Bloomington, IN
Louisville	Louisville, KY
Temple	Philadelphia, PA
Notre Dame	Notre Dame, IN
DePaul	Chicago, IL
Stanford	Stanford, CA
Connecticut	Storrs, CT
Louisiana State	Baton Rouge, LA
Texas Tech	Lubbock, TX
Univ. of Michigan	Ann Arbor, MI
USC	Los Angeles, CA
Michigan State	East Lansing, MI
Georgetown	Washington, DC
Cincinnati	Cincinnati, OH
Wisconsin	Madison, WI
Gonzaga	Spokane, WA
Oklahoma	Norman, OK

Directions: Colleges have created some colorful names for the teams that represent them. See how many of these nicknames you can match with the colleges listed above.

Blue Devils	Cornhuskers	Running Rebels	Trojans
Bruins	Fighting Irish	Sooners	Volunteers
Bulldogs	Hoyas	Spartans	Wildcats
Cardinal	Razorbacks	Tar Heels	Wolverines

Social Studies/Geography

Olympic Basketball

Men's basketball became an official Olympic sport in 1936. Forty years later women's basketball became an Olympic event. Listed below are some of the countries that have basketball teams in the Olympics.

Directions: Use a world map or atlas to help you complete the following activities.
1. Indicate the continent where the nation is located.
2. Label each of these countries on the world map on the next page.
3. If the country is very small, draw an arrow with the name of the country next to it.

Olympic Basketball Nations   **Continent**
1. United States   _____
2. Canada   _____
3. Italy   _____
4. Brazil   _____
5. Spain   _____
6. France   _____
7. Croatia   _____
8. Russia   _____
9. Korea   _____
10. Bulgaria   _____
11. China   _____
12. Thailand   _____
13. Philippines   _____
14. Switzerland   _____
15. Chile   _____
16. Lithuania   _____
17. Czechoslovakia   _____
18. Cuba   _____
19. Australia   _____
20. Zaire   _____

Express Your Opinion

In the last few years, the International Olympic Committee has changed its rules so that professional athletes can participate in the games. Before this change, only amateur athletes, who had never been directly paid to play, were allowed to participate. Countries could support a team, however. The new rules allowed Michael Jordan and other professional basketball players to create a "Dream Team," which often crushed teams from other nations.

> Write a persuasive essay expressing your opinions about using professionals in the Olympics. Be sure to include a topic sentence, three reasons to support your opinion, and a concluding statement.

Social Studies/Geography

Olympic Basketball *(cont.)*
World Map

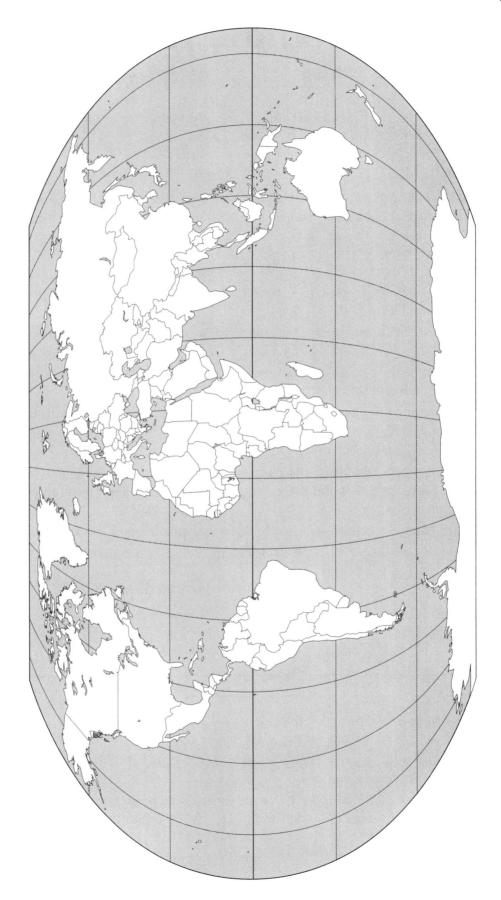

© Teacher Created Materials, Inc. 61 #3103 Thematic Unit—Basketball

Social Studies/Geography

Research the NBA Greats

Research Guidelines

Directions: Use these guidelines to find important information about your player. Use the tips at the bottom of the page to help you write your report.

I. Youth

Birthdate; places lived during youth; family—parents, siblings; home life—(farm/town) (rich/poor) (important events); education—from grade school to high school; activities and hobbies during childhood; childhood heroes

II. Adult Life

Personal Information—marriage/children; college or higher education; adult hobbies and interests

Basketball Career—years played; positions played; teams played on

Performance—lifetime and best year statistics (field goals, free throws, rebounds, assists); special achievements; career highlights; playoff or championship games

Influence on the Game—reputation as a player; What made your player famous?

Greatest Challenge—Did your player have to overcome any obstacles, like injury, sickness, or racism?

Personality—Was he or she kind, gentle, or tough? Was your player a leader or a follower? How did he or she get along with players, fans, umpires, coaches, and managers?

Life After Basketball—jobs held after basketball career (on the court and off)

End of Life—date of death (if no longer living); cause of death

III. Personal Evaluation

What did you admire about your player? What was the most interesting thing he or she did? What questions would you ask your player?

Research Tips

- *Do the research*—Find out everything you can about your sports figure. Discover the important dates, vital statistics, and facts about your player's personal life and struggles.
- *Go to the sources*—Use encyclopedias, almanacs, biographies, the Internet, and other sources to acquire the information you need.
- *Take careful notes*—Use your own words. Write down basic facts in an orderly way. Look for anecdotes and funny stories about your player. Become familiar with your player's accomplishments.
- *Write your report carefully*—Use your notes to write a detailed account of the life and career of your famous player.

Social Studies/Geography

Research the NBA Greats (cont.)

Famous Players

Directions: Select your famous player from the list below or choose one you are interested in.

Guards

Bob Cousy	A ball-handling magician
Clyde Drexler	Could jump over the moon, it seemed
Magic Johnson	Along with Bird, made the Final Four popular
Michael Jordan	"His Airness" did it all.
Oscar Robertson	Three players in one—shooter, playmaker, and small forward
John Stockton	The NBA's all-time leader in assists
Jerry West	A fierce competitor who had his nose broken nine times in his career

Forwards

Charles Barkley	A small forward with great power
Rick Barry	Best free throw shooter in NBA history
Elgin Baylor	An acrobat with a jump shot
Larry Bird	Great rebounder, shooter, and passer
Julius Erving	Great moves electrified fans
George Gervin	An ice cool shooter under pressure
Karl Malone	Mailman who always delivers for his team
Bob Pettit	Jump shooter extraordinaire
Scottie Pippin	A great player who played in Jordan's shadow
James Worthy	A true power forward on both ends of the court

Centers

Kareem Abdul-Jabbar	Had an awesome and unstoppable skyhook
Wilt Chamberlain	The greatest scorer ever
Patrick Ewing	A power player at both ends of the court
Moses Malone	In 21 years played for 10 clubs
George Mikan	The first of the great centers
Shaquille O'Neal	Simply dominates the paint
Hakeem Olajuwon	A great center who does it all
David Robinson	A role model on and off the court
Bill Russell	Led the Celtics in their glory days

Women Stars

Cynthia Cooper	First MVP in the new WNBA
Lisa Leslie	Los Angeles Sparks All Star
Nancy Lieberman	"Lady Magic"—college star at Old Dominion, Olympic player, WNBA coach
Rebecca Lobo	Star at UConn and WNBA Liberty
Cheryl Miller	Star at USC and the 1984 Olympics; WNBA coach
Ann Myers	First UCLA woman to get a full basketball scholarship
Sheryl Swoopes	Star at Texas Tech, the Olympics, and the NBA

Science

For Every Action . . .

For every action, there is an equal and opposite reaction.

The game of basketball is built on this principle of physics. Whether you are dribbling the ball, bouncing a pass to a teammate, or making a lay-up off the backboard, the ball is going to respond in predictable ways. You can do these activities with a classmate or by yourself.

Materials

a basketball, a backboard, and a solid wall or handball court

Directions

1. Bounce the ball on a hard, flat surface. Bounce it straight down. It should bounce directly back up. Use two hands. Try it with one hand. Dribble the ball by using the fingers of your hand to control the straight up and down movement.

2. Bounce the ball at an angle toward a teammate or a wall. Observe how the ball reacts after hitting the surface of the court. Bounce a pass at a teammate or a wall. Note how the bounce up is at the same angle as the bounce down. Try doing long, low bounce passes. Try short bounce passes.

3. Bounce the ball directly off a wall in front of you. Use two hands at first. It should come right back at you. Do this several times, then try bouncing the ball off the wall at different angles. Observe how the ball returns off the wall.

4. Bounce the ball off the backboard. Use two hands at first. Observe how the ball caroms off the board. Bounce the ball off many different parts of the board. Try to find one or two places where the ball goes off the backboard and through the net. Use one hand. Try the same activity with your other hand, the one you don't usually use.

Science

Dropping the Ball

Finding the right size of ball to use for basketball with the correct amount of bounce was one of the real problems for players when the game was young. Many changes and improvements were made along the way.

Materials

all types of balls—basketball, soccer ball, foam ball, baseball, rubber ball, football, etc. (borrow from other classes and/or ask students to bring balls in); a measuring stick (all yard or meter) for every three students

Directions

1. Place students in teams of three and assign the following duties: one student holds the measuring stick, one student drops the ball as instructed, and one student watches the ball and measuring stick and records how high the ball bounced.
2. Use as many balls as possible. Trade balls with other teams. You can use more than one of the same type of ball.
3. Drop each ball from a height of one measuring stick.
4. Record how high the ball bounced when it hit the ground. Do this three times with each ball and record on the chart the middle number or the number that appeared more than once. Which ball bounced highest?

Dropping Chart

Type of Ball	Height of Bounce

Two Dropped Balls

In the first experiment, no ball bounced higher than the measuring stick. In this experiment, you will drop two balls at exactly the same time to see what happens.

Materials

measuring sticks, basketballs, tennis balls, other small rubber balls (handballs, balls from jacks, etc.)

Directions

1. Use teams of three as in the previous activity except that the student dropping the ball will keep the tennis ball balanced on top of the basketball and drop them both straight down.
2. The student watching and recording must notice how high the tennis ball bounces.
3. Do this activity several times using different smaller balls.

What Happened

When you dropped the two balls together, the energy from the basketball was transferred to the smaller ball. The tennis ball was bouncing with the energy from both balls.

Health/P.E.

Setting the Offense

Team strategy is important in basketball. The diagrams below show two offensive formations (arrangement of players on the court) used as the team approaches the basket in an attempt to score a goal. Some player positions are identified in the diagrams and defined below.

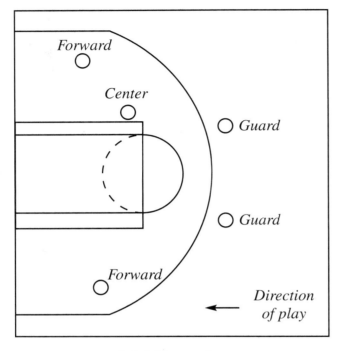
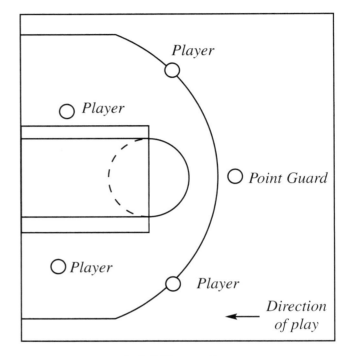

2-1-2 Formation **1-2-2 Formation**

Player Positions

- The *point guard* brings the ball up the court. He is generally the best ball handler (dribbling and passing) and often the quickest player on the team. Many times he is the shortest player. He is the team quarterback. He sets up the plays.

- The *shooting guard* (or off guard) is also a capable ball handler and the team's best long distance shooter. He is often the top scorer on the team.

- The *small forward* is a versatile player who can shoot at either long or short range, rebound, block shots, and pass the ball effectively. Often he is the most athletic player on the team. He is small only by comparison to the other forward and the center.

- The *power forward* is a good rebounder, an excellent defensive player, and a competent shooter at close range.

- The *center* is usually the team's tallest player. He plays close to the basket and is excellent at rebounding, blocking shots, and shooting near the basket with hook shots, tip-ins, slam-dunks, or lay-ups.

- The bench usually has about seven *reserve players*, often chosen for special abilities such as three-point shooting, tough defensive play, rebounding skills, or the ability to draw fouls from opposing players. The sixth man is the best reserve player and often gets a good deal of playing time.

Health/P.E.

Dribbling the Ball

The three essential skills of basketball are *dribbling*, *passing*, and *shooting*. You will learn how to dribble on this page. Good dribbling and passing skills will enable you to move around on the court and score. Passing skills and shooting techniques will be addressed on the following pages.

How to Dribble

1. Control the ball with the fingers. Cup the hand so that the fingertips, not the palm, are pushing down on the ball.

2. Spread the fingers so that they cover quite a large area on the ball.

3. Bend over slightly when dribbling, keeping the knees slightly bent. Avoid standing straight up.

4. Keep the bounce of the dribble at waist height. It is harder to steal the ball this way.

Dribbling Drills

Two-line Fast Dribbling

1. Set up two lines of equal size with the students facing each other.

2. The lines should be about 10 to 12 feet (3 to 3.65 m) apart.

3. The first player in line A dribbles the ball to the first player in line B and then lines up behind line B.

4. The player in line B who received the dribble, dribbles the ball back to the next player in line A and lines up behind line A.

5. Each player should be dribbling and running about every minute.

Half-court Dribble/Full-court Dribble

- As players become more adept, increase the distance to half the length of a basketball court and then the entire length of the court.

- Individual dribbling drills could also include dribbling the entire perimeter of the court or half of the court.

- Encourage students to practice slow dribbling, changing the direction of their dribbling, and dribbling with either hand.

© Teacher Created Materials, Inc.

Health/P.E.

Passing the Ball

Passing the ball is throwing the ball from one teammate to another. These passes should be done in teams of two players. Use several basketballs, if possible, or have teams practice the passes taking turns for one minute.

Two-handed Chest Pass (basic pass)
1. Hold the ball chest high with the fingers spread apart on both sides of the ball.
2. Push the ball away from the chest with a snap of the wrists.
3. Throw the ball straight and hard at your teammate.

Two-handed Bounce Pass
1. Aim the ball at a spot on the floor about two-thirds or three-fourths of the distance from you to your teammate.
2. Take one step toward the spot as you throw.
3. Practice until the pass bounces about waist high at your partner. (If the ball is too low or too high, it is harder for your partner to control it and easier for the opponent to steal it.)

Two-handed Overhead Pass
1. Hold the ball over your head with the fingers spread apart on both sides of the ball.
2. Step toward your teammate as you throw.
3. Pushing the ball away with a snap of the wrists.
4. Throw the ball straight and hard at your teammate.

Baseball Pass (a fast-break pass designed to travel most of the length of the court)
1. Hold the ball behind your ear fairly close to your head.
2. Snap your wrist down as you throw the ball.
3. Aim the ball three or four steps ahead of your teammate if he is running.
4. Lob the ball in a high arc if your teammate is already positioned near the basket.

Passing Drills
Two-line Fast Passing
1. Follow the procedures as in Two-line Fast Dribbling (page 67) but pass the ball instead.

Passing on the Wall
Sometimes, you just don't have a partner with whom to play ball. In basketball, you can not only practice shooting alone but passing and rebounding, as well. All you need is a wall or a backboard.
1. Use two small pieces of tape to make an X on the wall about chest high.
2. Stand five feet away from the X and practice the two-handed chest pass 20 times. The best passes will hit on or near the X and bounce almost directly back to you.
3. Increase the distance to 10 feet and throw another 20 passes. Try this again at 15 feet (4.6 m) and then 20 feet (6 m).
4. Try using a bounce pass from 12 or 15 feet (3.65 or 4.6 m) away. Aim at a spot on the blacktop about two-thirds or three-fourths of the way to the wall. Try to hit the X. Practice at different distances. Try throwing the ball with greater force or reducing the force.
5. Try hitting the X with the two-handed overhead throw. Try it at different distances.

Board Work
Use a backboard for this drill and concentrate on one spot, which is away from the basket.
1. Use two hands over your head to toss the ball at that spot.
2. Rebound the ball and keep trying to hit the same spot. Do this 20 times.
3. Hit the same spot again. Grab the ball and take one shot. Do this 20 times.

Health/P.E.

Shooting the Ball

Shooting the ball requires lots of practice. Practice several shots of each type before you go on to the next shot.

Set Shot
1. Right-handers should have the right foot two or three inches in front of the left. (Reverse the feet for left-handed shooters.)
2. Face the basket with your weight evenly distributed on both feet.
3. Hold the ball in one hand by the fingers as you shoot—not the palm of the hand.
4. Hold the other hand on the side of the ball to guide the shot.
5. Keep the knees slightly bent and push up with your legs.
6. Push the ball straight off your fingers. Fully extend your elbow.
7. Pull your wrist down as you finish the shot.

Bank Shot—Use the same basic form as with the set shot. Aim for one spot on the backboard a little above and to the side of the basket. The ball should bounce off the spot and into the basket. Practice until you have found the right spot on the backboard.

Jump Shot—Use the same basic form as with the set shot. Jump straight up into the air. Bring the ball into position and shoot.

Spot Shots—Choose one spot on the court. Take 10 shots from this one spot. Use the same basic form as with the set shot. Choose different spots to try. Become an expert at shooting from certain places on the court.

Two-handed Set Shot—Use this shot if you have trouble shooting the ball and reaching the basket. Use the same basic form as with the set shot except hold the ball with two hands above and to each side of the ball. Bend both elbows and push off with both arms like a two-handed chest pass.

Basic Lay-ups—A lay-up is a shot where the player dribbles close to the basket and shoots the ball against the backboard into the basket. Right-handers should dribble and shoot from the right side of the basket, left-handers from the left side. Right-handers should try to bring the right hand, arm, and leg up at the same time as he or she pushes off with the left leg. The reverse is true for left-handers.

Basketball Relay

For this game, use one basketball for each line.
1. Form two lines of students. The lines should be at half court.
2. The first player in each line dribbles down the court and makes a shot.
3. Whether the player makes the basket or not, he or she grabs the rebound and throws the ball down the court to the next player in line.
4. The team making the most number of baskets wins.

You can turn this into a game of one-on-one by using one basketball and having each team take turns being the offensive players (the players with possession of the ball). Reverse roles when everyone on one team has had a shot. The defensive players try to prevent the other team from scoring by stealing the ball, knocking the ball out of bounds, or blocking the shot.

Shooting Games

Around the World

This game can be played with two or more players.

There are seven positions around the free throw lane.

- The first is just to the right of the basket on the edge of the lane.
- The second is midway up to the foul line.
- The third is at the corner of the foul line.
- The fourth is at the middle of the foul line.
- The fifth is at the opposite corner.
- The sixth is midway down the opposite side of the line.
- The seventh is just to the left of the basket.

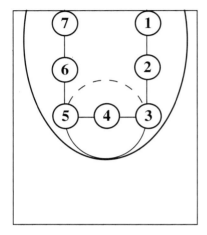

To Play the Game

1. All players start at the first position.
2. If you shoot and miss, you stay at that position until your turn comes again.
3. If you make the shot, you move to the next position. You continue to move "Around the World" until you miss a shot.
4. The winner is the player who makes the shots from all seven positions.

Horse

This game can be played with two or more players.

To Play the Game

1. The first player takes a shot from anywhere on the court. If he makes the shot, every other player must shoot from the same, exact spot. Other players who make the shot are not penalized but gain no points. Any player who misses that shot gets an H.
2. The first player can choose wherever he wants to shoot from, as long as he makes his shot.
3. When the first player misses his shot, the second player may choose where he wants to shoot from. If the second player makes his shot, everyone must shoot from his position. This continues for all the players.
4. Every time a player misses a shot set by another player, he gets another letter.
5. The process continues until one player has spelled H-O-R-S-E. He is the loser. The player with the fewest letters is the winner.
6. For a shorter version of the game, try B-U-G. For a longer version, try R-H-I-N-O-C-E-R-O-S.

Health/P.E.

Base Basketball

Base Basketball reinforces two important basketball skills: *passing* and *shooting*. It is played on a basketball court with the entire class divided into two even teams.

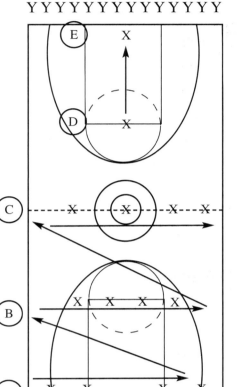

Setting Up the Game

The offensive team (**X**) is divided evenly into three lines. One line is positioned along the end line (**A**). The next line is stationed along the free throw line (**B**). The third line is stationed on the center court line (**C**). All lines face the basket at the opposite end of the court. The player at the far right of line C goes to the basket and stands under it (**E**) facing his team. He is the rebounder. The next player on the far right of line C goes to the free throw line (**D**) and faces the basket. He is the first shooter.

The defensive team (**Y**) is lined up behind the end line at the left corner of the court.

Getting Started

The offensive team has one minute from the time the defensive player puts the ball into play to make a basket. The first defensive player throws the ball the full length of the court to the offensive players lined up along the other end line (**A**).

Playing the Game

One offensive player along line A grabs the ball and throws it to any player along line B. That player throws the ball to any player along line C. Then that player throws it to the shooter who then takes his first shot from the free throw line. The rebounder grabs the ball and throws it back to the shooter, who can take a shot from any place on the court. He shoots as often as he can until he makes a basket or time is up.

Scoring the Game

If the shooter makes the basket, the offensive team scores two points. If he fails, his team has one out. The offensive team changes places with the defensive team when it gets three outs.

Rotating the Shooter

After the minute is up, the rebounder goes to the left side of line A. The shooter becomes the rebounder. The player at the far right of line C becomes the next shooter. Each player on each line moves one place to the right. The players on the far right of lines A and B move up to the left of lines B and C, respectively. The team continues to rotate in this zigzag fashion.

The first defensive player moves to the end of his line and the next player puts the ball into play.

Notes and Tips

- Only the designated shooter gets credit for a score.
- The ball is in bounds if it touches any part of the court or any player.
- If the defensive player throws the ball out of bounds, the offensive team gets one point and the next defensive player puts the ball into play.
- If the defensive player throws the ball short or too low and an offensive player on line B intercepts the ball, it can be thrown to line C immediately, and then to the shooter. If a player on line C intercepts the ball, it can be thrown directly to the shooter.
- If an offensive player drops the ball, it must be retrieved by him and thrown up the lines as usual.

Health/P.E.

Basketball Etiquette

The Blame Game

Daren McCall played the "blame game." When things went wrong, someone else was always to blame. Lou wasn't playing well so the Ranger losses were Lou's fault. When Gary didn't catch onto dribbling, it was Gary's fault. When Lynn tried to tell Daren the truth, Daren cut him off and nearly lost a friend.

Daren needed to learn sportsmanship. When he started accepting responsibility and stopped blaming his teammates, the Rangers started to win.

Michael Jordan was the best player for the Bulls for several years before he learned that not only did he have to be good, he had to lead his team and make them better. He had to learn to be unselfish on and off the court.

Even though Buzz knew that the referee seemed to make bad calls against the Blazers, he didn't let himself or his team get upset. He taught them how to overcome their adversity.

Tipper and the Fast Breakers beat Courtney's Blue Stars because Tipper insisted that everyone have an opportunity to practice and play in the game. She didn't favor just one or two players.

Here are some things you can do to demonstrate good sportsmanship on and off the basketball court.

Self Control Tips

- Remember that it is only a game. No matter how badly you want to win, it is only a game. Don't lose friends and the respect of your teammates by losing your temper.
- Stop. Count to 10. Get control of your breathing and your body.
- Think before you speak. When you do speak, be reasonable, clear, and honest about your opinions.
- Don't expect to convince others. Right or wrong, other people aren't always going to agree with you.
- Respect the opinions of others. You don't have to change your mind but do recognize that others have a right to a different opinion.
- Respect others. Don't insult, hit, or lash out at other people. They have feelings, too.
- Life isn't always fair. Sometimes the breaks of the game or the umpire's call go someone else's way. Learn to accept it.

Leadership Tips

- Think "we" not "me." There is no "I" in team. The team comes first.
- Pass the ball around. In basketball, one player is only a part of the effort. He's not going to win the game alone—even if he is the best player. Nobody likes a ball hog.
- Give everyone a chance to play. Nobody gets better without a chance to practice and play.
- Be fair. Teammates may admire the shooting of a great player but they respect fairness even more.
- Don't show off. There's no place for a clown on the court.

Creative Writing

Describe a time when you really lost your temper. It may have been during a game or some other event. Describe how the tips above might have helped you handle the situation.

Role Playing

Work with a partner on this activity. Set up a situation where you both get into an argument over a foul situation, an out-of-bounds call, a violation of the rules, a missed shot, or some other basketball situation. Role-play the situation, then use the same situation and handle it in a mature and respectful way. Present both models to the class.

Art

Logos, Posters, and Uniforms

Logos

Design a logo for your favorite team: your school team, a college team, an NBA team, or even an imaginary one. Create a distinctive, different, unusual design. Use bright colors. If your team already has a logo, improve it. Use this design to make a full-size logo on construction paper. Then send it to your favorite team.

Posters

Design a basketball poster to advertise your favorite team. Sketch out your design on the back of this paper and then use it to make a full size poster on butcher paper. Send the poster to your favorite team or add it to a bulletin board display in school.

Uniforms

Create your own design for a uniform to be worn by your favorite team. Choose the colors to be worn. Decide where you want to place the name of the team, the name of the player, and the player's number. Consider changing the style of the uniform such as longer sleeves or shorter pants, as well.

Extension
- Brainstorm some ideas for souvenirs and create one of them!
- Write about the souvenir you developed and suggest it in a letter to the team you designed it for.

Culminating Activity

The Final Four

The Final Four is the most prestigious event in college basketball. The NCAA tournament starts out with 64 competing teams and gets down to the final weekend with only four teams left to vie for the championship.

Declare a specific day as Final Four Day. Follow these suggestions to ensure a day of success.

1. Divide your class into four teams of equal ability. Each team should have five to eight players. Be sure that all students have an opportunity to play.

2. Have each team choose a color of T-shirt for it's team to wear. Students who have basketball uniforms can wear them over their T-shirt.

3. In keeping with the basketball theme of the day, consider a luncheon with a basketball motif. Enlist several parents to help with the cooking and organization.

4. Set aside a long afternoon period for the games among the "final four." Try to get a parent or high school student to referee each game. Set up a semi-final game between the two sets of two teams. Select timekeepers and scorekeepers from students who are unable to play due to injury or special needs. Limit the games to 30 minutes. Have a 20-minute playoff game between the two winning teams.

5. Award Team Player Certificates (page 77) to all students who participate.

6. Take pictures and create a bulletin board display that celebrates Final Four Day.

Final Four Day is Here!

Dear _____,

We are planning a day of celebration as we complete our Basketball unit. Can you help us prepare our luncheon? Please fill out the information below and return it by _____.

I can prepare the following food:
_____
_____

I can donate the following items (paper products, drinks, etc.):
_____

Parent Name: _____ Phone #: _____

#3103 Thematic Unit—Basketball

Bulletin Board Ideas

Yesterday and Today

Display the uniform designs that students drew and colored. Have students use the Internet or appropriate resource books to find examples of uniforms and equipment worn in basketball's early days. Display alongside their original drawings.

Heroes of the Game

Ask students to cut out pictures of favorite players from sports magazines. They can also use pictures from basketball books that have been enlarged on a copy machine. Post the pictures and label them. This is a good kick-off for the social studies research activities highlighted in this book. Each student could post a picture of his player and a copy of his report.

Additional Ideas

- *Highlight the Books*—Encourage your students to choose their favorite scenes from any of the three literature selections. Ask students to illustrate these scenes with simple line drawings, colored pencils, markers, or any other available media. Post this student artwork.
- *Logos and Posters*—When students have finished designing their logos and posters for their favorite teams, create a display of them in a collage format.

Unit Management

Bulletin Board Ideas *(cont.)*

Basketball Word Wall

Create a bulletin board panel with many of the basketball words and phrases highlighted in **Basketball Terms** (page 47) and **Basketball Lingo** (page 48). Write the words on sentence strips.

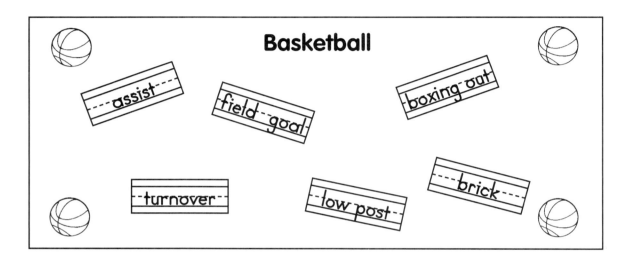

Geography Lives

Post a large map of the United States and Canada. Ask students to locate each city and state on the map with a flag sign for each team. You can also do a similar bulletin board with a map of the world, asking students to flag the countries where Olympic basketball is played. Use an Olympic motif.

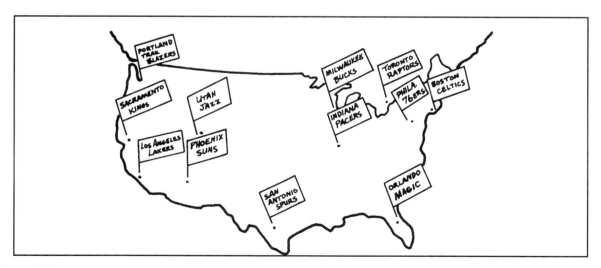

Additional Ideas

- *Poetry on the Wall*—Have students place their poems on a panel. Ask each student to create an illustration to go with his or her poem to add color and dynamic effect to the presentation.
- *Final Four*—Take pictures at your Final Four Day and display them, possibly mixed in with a collage of action shots of NBA players.

Unit Management

Team Player Certificate

Coach's Basketball Award

"There's No 'I' in Team"

This award is presented to

_____

in recognition of exceptional

Team Spirit ★ Leadership ★ Initiative

Signed: _____

Date: _____

Bibliography

Fiction

Dadey, Debbie and Jones, Marcia Thornton. *Leprechauns Don't Play Basketball* (Bailey School Kids Series #4). Scholastic, Inc., 1992.

Dubowski, Cathy. *The Case of the Slam Dunk Mystery* (New Adventures of Mary-Kate and Ashley Series). HarperCollins Children's Books, 2000.

Fitzgerald, John D. *The Great Brain at the Academy.* Dial, 1972.

Myers, Walter Dean. *Hoops.* Bantam Doubleday Dell Books for Young Readers, 1983.

Soto, Gary. *Taking Sides.* Harcourt, 1992.

Nonfiction

Boomerangs, Blades, & Basketballs: The Science of Sports (Science@Work Series). Raintree, Steck-Vaughn Publishers, 2000.

Kirkpatrick, Rob. *Michael Jordan: Basketball Superstar.* The Rosen Publishing Group, Inc., 2000.

Kramer, Sydelle A. *Basketball's Great Players* (Step into Reading Series). Random House, 1997.

Lannin, Joanne. *A History of Basketball for Girls and Women: From Bloomers to Big Leagues.* Lerner Sports, 2000.

Lovitt, Chip. *Michael Jordan.* Scholastic, 1995.

Mullin, Chris. *The Young Basketball Player.* Dorling Kindersley, 1995.

Pietrusza, David. *Michael Jordan.* Lucent Books, 1998.

Roberts, Robin. *Basketball Year, Get in the Game!* Millbrook Press, 2000.

Sachare, Alex. *The Basketball Hall of Fame's Hoop Facts and Stats: Records and Stories from the Naismith Memorial Basketball Hall of Fame.* John Wiley & Sons, 1997.

Smith, Michelle. *She's Got Game: Stars of the WNBA.* Scholastic, Inc., 1999.

Vancil, Mark. *NBA Basketball Basics.* Sterling Publishing Co., 1995.

Picture Books

Jordan, Deloris and Jordan, Roslyn M. *Salt in His Shoes: Michael Jordan in Pursuit of a Dream.* Simon & Schuster, 2000.

Martin, Bill. *Swish!* Henry Holt Books for Young Readers, 2000.

Marzollo, Jean. *Slam Dunk Saturday* (Stepping-Stone Books). Random House Books for Young Readers, 1994.

Mayers, Florence C. *Basketball ABC: The NBA Alphabet.* Harry N. Abrams, Inc., 1996.

Poetry

Adoff, Arnold. *The Basket Counts.* Simon & Schuster Books for Young Readers, 2000.

Glenn, Mel. *Jump Ball: A Basketball Season in Poems.* Dutton Children's Books, 1997.

Hopkins, Lee Bennett. *Opening Days: Sports Poems.* Harcourt Brace & Company, 1996.

Slam Dunk: Poems About Basketball. Hyperion Books for Children, 1995.

Internet Websites

www.nba.com

www.InsideHoops.com

Bibliography (cont.)

Other books by Matt Christopher

This is a selected list of Matt Christopher's most popular books. All are published by Little, Brown and Company.

Fiction

Basketball Sparkplug, 1957.
Break for the Basket, 1960.
Center Court Sting, 1998.
Johnny Long Legs, 1988.
Red Hot Hightops (Sports Classics Series #30), 1992.
Shoot for the Hoop (Sports Classics Series #43), 1995.
The Basket Counts, 1991.
Wheel Wizards, 2000.

Nonfiction

On the Court with . . . Grant Hill, 1996.
On the Court with . . . Hakeem Olajuwon, 1998.
On the Court with . . . Lisa Leslie, 1998.
On the Court with . . . Michael Jordan, 1996.

Other Sports

All Star Fever, 1995.
Baseball Flyhawk, 1963.
Centerfield Ballhawk, 1992.
Fighting Tackle, 1995.
Johnny No Hit, 1978.
No Arm in Left Field, 1974.
Return of the Home Run Kid, 1992.
Skateboard Tough, 1991.
Soccer Halfback, 1978.
The Catcher with a Glass Arm, 1964.
The Hockey Machine, 1986.
The Kid Who Only Hit Homers, 1972.
The Lucky Baseball Bat, 1991.
The Winning Stroke, 1994.
Too Hot to Handle, 1965.
Top Wing, 1994.

The Boxcar Children Books

This is a selected list of the Boxcar Children books created by Gertrude Chandler Warner and written by various authors. All of the books, published by Albert Whitman & Company, are listed in the order in which they were written.

The Boxcar Children, 1942. (The original)
Surprise Island, 1949.
The Yellow House Mystery, 1953.
Mystery Ranch, 1958.
Mike's Mystery, 1960.
Blue Bay Mystery, 1961.
Woodshed Mystery, 1962.
The Lighthouse Mystery, 1963.
The Mountain Top Mystery, 1964.
The Schoolhouse Mystery, 1965.
The Caboose Mystery, 1966.
Mystery Behind the Wall, 1973.
Houseboat Mystery, 1990.
The Deserted Library Mystery, 1991.
The Animal Shelter Mystery, 1991.
Bus Station Mystery, 1991.
Benny Uncovers a Mystery, 1991.
The Haunted Cabin Mystery, 1991.
The Mystery of the Mixed-Up Zoo, 1992.
The Mystery of the Hidden Painting, 1992.
The Old Motel Mystery, 1992.
The Mystery Girl, 1992.
The Camp-Out Mystery, 1992.
The Disappearing Friend, 1992.
The Mystery Cruise, 1992.
The Mystery in the Snow, 1993.
The Castle Mystery, 1993.
The Mystery Horse, 1993.
The Pizza Mystery, 1993.
The Mystery of the Stolen Boxcar, 1995.
The Mystery of the Hot Air Balloon, 1995.
The Panther Mystery, 1995.
The Dinosaur Mystery, 1995.
The Basketball Mystery, 1996.
The Guide Dog Mystery, 1996.
The Ghost Town Mystery, 1997.
The Mystery in the Mall, 1999.
The Mystery of the Pirate's Map, 1999.
The Great Bicycle Race Mystery, 2000.
The Summer Camp Mystery, 2001.
The Mystery of the Midnight Dog, 2001.

Answer Key

Page 17
1. B   3. D   5. B   7. A   9. D
2. B   4. B   6. B   8. A   10. D

Page 20
1. still in effect
2. changed
3. partly in effect
4. still in effect
5. first two parts still in effect
6. still in effect
7. changed
8. mostly still in effect
9. changed
10. changed
11. mostly still in effect
12. changed
13. first part still in effect

Page 34
1. C   3. C   5. D   7. B   9. B
2. D   4. B   6. A   8. A   10. B

Page 49

Bird	24.3	Robertson	25.7
Baylor	27.4	Abdul-Jabbar	24.6
Malone	25.9	O'Neal	27.7
Olajuwon	22.5	West	27.0
Ewing	21.8	Maravich	24.2
Chamberlain	30.1	Thompson	22.1
Jordan	31.5	Barkley	22.1
Erving	22.0		

1. Michael Jordan   3. Kareem Abdul-Jabbar
2. Kareem Abdul-Jabbar

Page 50
1. 288 ft. (87.8 m)
2. 4,700 sq. ft. (436 m^2)
3. 70 ft. (21 m)
4. 304 sq. ft. (28 m^2)
5. 37.68 ft. (11.48 m)
6. 12.56 ft. (3.8 m)
7. 113.04 sq. ft. (10.5 m^2)
8. 12.56 sq. ft. (1.17 m^2)

Page 51
1. Kevin Garnett
2. $324,285
3. $4,750,000
4. $29,415,715
5. $89,375,715
6. $2,540,000
7. They made the same amount.
8. $190,345,715
9. $13,596,122.50
10. Scottie Pippin

Page 52
1. 38%   3. 50%   5. 49%   7. 46%
2. 39%   4. 57%   6. 41%   8. 48%

Page 53
1. .683   5. .500   9. .671   13. .378
2. .585   6. .610   10. .646   14. .439
3. .683   7. .646   11. .305   15. .707
4. .183   8. .488   12. .573   16. .207

1. San Antonio   2. Indiana
3. Utah and Dallas (.646), Philadelphia and Lakers (.683)

Page 56

Atlanta Hawks	Georgia
Boston Celtics	Massachusetts
Charlotte Hornets	North Carolina
Chicago Bulls	Illinois
Cleveland Cavaliers	Ohio
Dallas Mavericks	Texas
Denve Nuggets	Colorado
Detroit Pistons	Michigan
Golden State Warriors	California
Houston Rockets	Texas
Indiana Pacers	Indiana
Los Angeles Clippers	California
Los Angeles Lakers	California
Miami Heat	Florida
Milwaukee Bucks	Wisconsin
Minnesota Timberwolves	Minnesota
New Jersey Nets	New Jersey
New York Knicks	New York
Orlando Magic	Florida
Philadelphia 76ers	Pennsylvania
Phoenix Suns	Arizona
Portland Trail Blazers	Oregon
Sacramento Kings	California
San Antonio Spurs	Texas
Seattle Supersonics	Washington
Toronto Raptors	Ontario, Canada
Utah Jazz	Utah
Vancouver Grizzlies	British Columbia, Canada
Washington Wizards	District of Columbia

1. 20   3. 14   5. California   7. 4
2. 2   4. 15   6. 30   8. 3

Page 59

Duke Blue Devils	UNLV Running Rebels
UCLA Bruins	Oklahoma Sooners
Gonzaga Bulldogs	Michigan State Spartans
Stanford Cardinal	North Carolina Tar Heels
Nebraska Cornhuskers	USC Trojans
Notre Dame Fighting Irish	Tennessee Volunteers
Georgetown Hoyas	Kentucky Wildcats
Arkansas Razorbacks	Michigan Wolverines

Page 60
1. North America   11. Asia
2. North America   12. Asia
3. Europe   13. Asia
4. South America   14. Europe
5. Europe   15. South America
6. Europe   16. Europe
7. Europe   17. Europe
8. Europe/Asia   18. North America
9. Asia   19. Australia
10. Europe   20. Africa